The Cross Through the Open Tomb

BOOKS BY DONALD GREY BARNHOUSE

The Cross
through the
Open Tomb

by

DONALD GREY BARNHOUSE

WILLIAM B. EERDMANS PUBLISHING COMPANY

GRAND RAPIDS, MICHIGAN

Quotations from the Revised Standard Version of the Bible, copyright 1946, 1952, by the Division of Christian Education of the National Council of Churches, are used by permission of Thomas Nelson & Sons, New York. Quotations from The New Testament in Modern English, translated by J. B. Phillips, are used by permission of The Macmillan Company, New York.

Τῷ ἀγαπῶντι ἡμᾶς καὶ λύσαντι
ἡμᾶς ἐκ τῶν ἁμαρτιῶν ἡμῶν
ἐν τῷ αἵματι αὐτοῦ.

Rev. 1:5

PREFACE

As the title indicates, the purpose of this book is to set forth the death of the Lord Jesus Christ in the light of His resurrection. Too often even evangelical believers think that the climactic event in the life of the Lord Jesus was His death. It was not. Rather, it was His resurrection. To be sure, He had to die in order to forgive our sins and justify us before God. But had He not risen from the grave, we could not have eternal life, nor could we live a life of holiness in a sinful world.

We have a risen Savior who is our living contemporary. He has not only saved us for heaven but He is able to bring heaven into our souls as we daily walk with Him in the power of His risen life. Our desire is that of the Apostle Paul, who wrote to the Philippians: "That I may know him, and the power of his resurrection, and the fellowship of his sufferings, being made conformable unto his death; if by any means I might attain unto the out-resurrection [Gk.] from among the dead" (Phil. 3:10, 11).

May the Holy Spirit cause the Risen Christ to become a reality in your daily life!

—DONALD GREY BARNHOUSE

7

CONTENTS

9

CONTENTS

RISEN FROM THE TOMB
"Now Is Christ Risen from the Dead"

In the five studies of Part One we present the fact that Jesus Christ did rise from the tomb, that He truly is the Risen Lord of Glory with whom we are identified through the new birth.

Chapter One

RISEN FROM THE TOMB

Have you ever looked at the cross of our Lord Jesus Christ through the open tomb? Have you ever gone back to Calvary by way of the resurrection? To me it is unfortunate that we approach the cross of Jesus Christ as though it were the climax of His life instead of a great episode that led to the much greater event of the resurrection and all that followed it. The Apostle Paul did not know the cross from the incarnation side but from the resurrection side. Indeed, he wrote to the Corinthians, "Yea, though we have known Christ after the flesh, yet now henceforth know we him no more" (2 Cor. 5:16). Every Christian needs to see Christ from the resurrection side of Calvary. We must see Him through the open tomb.

In the time of the Apostle Paul, believers did not read the four Gospels, for the Gospels had not yet been written. Paul never heard John 3:16. "For God so loved the world, that he gave his only begotten Son, that whosoever believeth in him should not perish, but have everlasting life."

13

The Gospels were written for that generation of believers who never knew Jesus Christ in the flesh, who knew Him only through the epistles of Paul. The Gospels were written under the Holy Spirit's direction so that the Church might know more about our Lord. That is why we find verses in the epistles that are far more significant than some verses in the Gospels. The Gospels tell us *that* Jesus Christ died on the cross. The epistles explain *why* Jesus Christ died on the cross and why it was necessary for Him to rise from the dead.

The early believers approached the Gospels through the epistles; they approached the earthly life of Christ from the point of view of His present heavenly life; they approached the cross through the open tomb.

I believe it is not wise to teach the crucifixion as the climax of the life of Christ. Such teaching not only minimizes the resurrection, but it also robs the believer of a sense of the ever-living presence of his Lord in daily life.

As we approach the cross from the resurrection side, through the open tomb, let us consider it in three aspects: First, what the cross means in relation to our past sins; second, what it means in our present daily life; and third, what it means in relation to our future hope. Reflecting on these things, we shall be filled with great joy.

First, as we think of the cross in connection with our past sin, we shall know only sorrowing defeat unless we see the death of Jesus Christ through the open tomb, for our sin nailed Jesus Christ to that cross. If we see Him merely dying, then there is nothing for us. But Christ arose from the grave, and His resurrection assures us that He has overcome death. The importance of this fact can be illustrated by an incident, well known in England, which took place after the Waterloo campaign of June, 1815. All England was awaiting news of the campaign in which the Duke of Wellington opposed Napoleon Bonaparte. Since it was long before the days of telegraph, watchers were stationed along the coast to catch semaphore signals from sailing vessels. Finally one watcher spied a sailing vessel beginning to wig-wag a message. The words were, "Wellington defeated." Then fog closed in. These words were relayed across England and all the nation was plunged into gloom. The fog then cleared and the message came through, "Wellington defeated the enemy." Sorrow was banished and all England rejoiced.

This story admirably illustrates what was the state of mind of people when Christ died. Jesus had claimed to be God. He had said, "The Son of man came to seek and to save that which was lost. I came not to be ministered unto but to minister, and to give my life a ransom for many." Then He was crucified. It was a terrible day. The sun was blotted from sight and there was darkness over the face of the earth. There was an earthquake. Events took place which caused even the Roman centurion to exclaim, "Truly this was the Son of God!" Then Christ died and His body was buried in the tomb of Joseph of Arimathea. The Pharisees smacked their lips and dusted their hands as if to say, "Well, that's that! We have gotten rid of this man who caused us so much trouble." Jesus defeated! Jesus defeated! Jesus defeated!

Then came the resurrection! The news was, "Jesus defeated the enemy!" He had vanquished death and all its power. And so today we can sing:

> My sin — O the bliss of this glorious thought! —
> My sin, not in part but the whole,
> Is nailed to the cross and I bear it no more;
> Praise the Lord, praise the Lord, O my soul!

Thus the resurrection of Jesus Christ gives us the triumphant cross. There our sin was dealt with; there our sin was paid for; there our enemy was defeated; there death with all its powers was vanquished and we have life in Christ. And so the Apostle Paul writes, "[Christ] was delivered from our offences, and was raised again for our justification. Therefore being justified by faith, we have peace with God through our Lord Jesus Christ" (Rom. 4:25—5:1). If you still harbor the fear of death, remember that the tomb is open. By rising from the dead, Christ robbed death of its sting, and so we can exult with the Apostle: "O death, where is thy sting? O grave, where is thy victory? The sting of death is sin; and the strength of sin is the law. But thanks be to God, which giveth us the victory through our Lord Jesus Christ" (1 Cor. 15:55-57).

Second, the cross through the tomb means that we have a living Savior, a Savior of our present daily life.

Years ago there was a missionary in Turkey who was having great difficulty making the Mohammedans understand why they should trust in Jesus Christ. One day he was traveling with some Moslems along an unmarked road when they came to a fork in the road. At this point there was the tomb of a Mohammedan "holy man." While they were trying to decide which fork to take, the missionary said, "Let's go to that tomb and ask the dead man." They all protested, "The dead man can give us no information! See that little house over there? Let's go there and ask a living man." "You are quite right," said the missionary. "Never forget that Mohammed is dead; he can give you no help or information; in him is no life. But Jesus Christ is alive, and He will give you eternal life if you will trust in Him as your Savior!"

Likewise, we do not approach a tomb that has the body of a dead man in it, as those who go to Mecca visit the tomb of Mohammed. The tomb of our Lord is empty and our Savior is in heaven interceding for us. This makes it possible for you and me to approach our risen Lord, for we read: "Since then we have a great high priest who has passed through the heavens, Jesus, the Son of God, let us hold fast our confession. For we have not a high priest who is unable to sympathize with our weaknesses, but one who in every respect has been tempted as we are, yet without sinning. Let us then with confidence draw near to the throne of grace, that we may receive mercy and find grace to help in time of need" (Heb. 4:14-16).

Furthermore, because Christ is risen, we have the high privilege of walking with Him in newness of life, for by His Spirit we are identified with Him, having been made partakers of His divine nature. This enables us to walk as the sons of God among the sons of men. Through the cross our sins are forgiven; by the open tomb the risen Lord imparts to us His eternal life. Thus Paul writes: "Do you not know that all of us who have been baptized into Christ Jesus were baptized into his death? We were buried therefore with him by baptism into death, so that as Christ was raised from the dead by the glory of the Father, we too might walk in newness of life" (Rom. 6:3, 4).

This new life in Christ is real and substantial and practical. God has given us His Holy Spirit in order that we may live daily the life of our risen Lord, as taught in His Word. Many believers do not appreciate this high privilege for two reasons: first, they do not study the Word of God to see the marks of His risen life; second, they are not willing to allow the Holy Spirit to work that life out through them because they prefer to serve their own sinful interests. This is why Paul writes, "To set the mind on the flesh is death, but to set the mind on the Spirit is life and peace. . . . For if you live according to the flesh you will die, but if by the Spirit you put to death the deeds of the body you will live. For all who are led by the Spirit of God are sons of God. For you did not receive the spirit of slavery to fall back into fear, but you have received the spirit of sonship. When we cry, 'Abba! Father!' it is the Spirit himself bearing witness with our spirit that we are children of God" (Rom. 8:6, 13-16).

When the cross is truly seen through the open tomb, we can be sure of victory in our risen Savior, amid the problems of daily life. God can tame our tongues; He can give us a word of grace instead of words of criticism. God can make us long-suffering instead of short-tempered. In all these things we can be more than conquerors through Him who loved us. Or do we prefer defeat? Do we prefer to indulge our old natures instead of letting the new nature prevail? Paul sums it up in that verse so well known but so little practiced: "I have been crucified with Christ; it is no longer I who live, but Christ who lives in me; and the life I now live in the flesh I live by faith in the Son of God, who loved me and gave himself for me" (Gal. 2:20).

God wants us to live daily the life of our risen Lord because we are to be His ambassadors: we present Christ to the lost. Just as a country cannot export a product which it does not produce, so we cannot demonstrate to the world a life that we do not live. But filled with the power of Christ's resurrection life and motivated by the love of God, we shall be true epistles of Christ, known and read by all men. Then as God's ambassadors, "the love of Christ controls us, because we are convinced that one has died for all; therefore all have died. And he died for all, that those who live might live no longer for themselves but for him who for their sake died and was raised" (2 Cor. 5:14, 15).

Perhaps you ask, "Can I really trust the risen Lord to direct my daily life?" I can answer this by the following incident. A college girl once said to me, "I have never trusted anyone in my life. How can I trust the Lord Jesus with all the problems of my daily life?" Since it was Easter vacation, I asked her how she was going to get back to college. She said, "I am going to fly." "Do you have your ticket?" I asked. "No," she said, "I have to find out what time I can get a plane." "How are you going to do that?" I inquired. "Well," she replied, "I am going to telephone the airline and find out what time the plane leaves and reserve a seat on that plane. Then I shall take a taxi out to the airport and board the plane." I said, "Do you know the reservation clerk at the airline?" She replied, "No, I don't." I asked, "Are you going to taxi to the airport trusting the information of this unknown clerk?" "Yes, I am." "Do you know the pilot of this plane?" "No, I don't." Then I said to her, "You trust the word of an unknown clerk at the airline office, and put your life into the hands of a pilot whom you do not know and probably will not even see. But you will know what real trust is when you take the word of the Lord Jesus Christ, who died for you and rose again, and allow Him to pilot your life by His resurrection power."

Third, not only is the cross through the open tomb our greatest triumph because our sins are forgiven and redeemed forever; not only do we have confidence and trust for daily life because our risen Lord is at the right hand of God; but the cross through the open tomb guarantees our future hope. Have you lost a loved one in death? What is your hope? Your hope is that Jesus Christ who died for your sins is alive. A mother had lost a son in the war; his body was never found and so he was reported missing in action. How wonderful that I could tell her, "That boy belongs to the Lord Jesus Christ. You can be sure that at the second coming of Christ the trumpet will locate him. When the Lord Jesus Christ says, 'Come forth!' that boy of yours will come forth from the grave, and you will be reunited forever." That is the hope of every child of God.

This is a glorious hope, especially when we realize that it is no figment of our imagination but the clear teaching of God's own Word: "Blessed be the God and Father of our Lord Jesus Christ! By his great mercy we have been born anew to a living hope through the resurrection of Jesus Christ from the dead, and to an inheritance which is imperishable, undefiled, and unfading, kept in heaven for you, who by God's power are guarded through faith for a salvation ready to be revealed in the last time" (1 Peter 1:3-5). Nothing can destroy this hope, nothing can corrupt it, nothing can defile it, nothing on earth can depreciate it, for this hope is reserved in heaven for us. Through the power of God we are being kept for this glorious hope. Nothing can keep us from it.

When the truth of this hope grips your heart, it will dominate your very life. The fear of death will vanish; the joy of living will be your portion. In fact, what the world calls death will be but the gateway to the full realization of the life which now we know in part. Thus Paul to the Philippian Church writes: "For to me to live is Christ, and to die is gain. If it is to be life in the flesh, that means fruitful labor for me. Yet which I shall choose I cannot tell. I am hard pressed between the two. My desire is to depart and be with Christ, for that is far better. But to remain in the flesh is more necessary on your account" (Phil. 1:21-24).

The open tomb transforms earthly sorrow into heavenly joy. How many of us have experienced the home-going of loved ones! Of course we sorrow, but we do not sorrow as the world does, for we look forward to that day when our blessed Lord will return, bringing our loved ones with Him. And so Paul writes to the Thessalonians: "But we would not have you ignorant, brethren, concerning those who are asleep, that you may not grieve as others do who have no hope. For since we believe that Jesus died and rose again, even so, through Jesus, God will bring with him those who have fallen asleep. . . . For the Lord himself will descend from heaven with a cry of command, with the archangel's call, and with the sound of the trumpet of God. And the dead in Christ will rise first; then we who are alive, who are left, shall be caught up together with them in the clouds to meet the Lord in the air; and so we shall always be with the Lord" (1 Thess. 4:13, 14, 16, 17).

In the light of these three reasons — past, present, and future — we can see why a bare cross, as a symbol of the Christian faith, is superior to a crucifix. The crucifix shows only the death of our Lord; it does not show the abundant, complete life promised by our risen Lord. As we see the bare cross through the open tomb, we glance away to heaven, where the God-Man who once died is now enthroned at the Father's side, waiting till all things are put under His feet.

Chapter Two

JESUS THE RISEN CHRIST

It may be that your study of the preceding chapter has opened your eyes to the glories of the cross when viewed from resurrection ground. But your experience might be similar to mine when, after the first flush of intense joy, I asked myself, "Did Jesus really rise from the dead?" How wonderful to be able to answer in the affirmative! In the first chapter of the epistle to the Romans, we read that the gospel concerns God's Son, the Lord Jesus Christ, "*descended* from David according to the flesh, and *designated* Son of God in power according to the Spirit of holiness by his resurrection from the dead" (vs. 3, 4).

We know that Christ rose from the dead, for there is the testimony of the Father recorded in the Word and testified to by the Holy Spirit.

Let us examine these words carefully. We find that there are two verbs concerning the coming of the Lord to earth. He was *descended* from David according to the flesh, and *designated* Son of God by the resurrection from the dead. His descent from David shows that the Lord Jesus Christ was truly man. His resurrection from the dead proves that He was truly God. *But we aren't — so a cold comfort*

21

There were many witnesses to the deity of Christ. Before looking at the facts which prove His deity, let us examine some witnesses who attest His deity. At His baptism, and again on the Mount of Transfiguration, God the Father testified, "This is my beloved Son in whom I am well pleased." Through the Apostle John the Holy Spirit testified, "Whoever confesses that Jesus is the Son of God, God abides in him, and he in God" (1 John 4:15). When the high priest asked Jesus, "Are you the Christ, the Son of the Blessed?" He replied, "I am; and you will see the Son of man sitting at the right hand of Power, and coming with the clouds of heaven" (Mark 14:61, 62).

Demons also acknowledged that Jesus was the Son of God. When He drove them out of the Gadarene maniacs they cried, "What have you to do with us, O Son of God?" (Matt. 8:29)! "And whenever the unclean spirits beheld him, they fell down before him and cried out, 'You are the Son of God' " (Mark 3:11).

Peter, James, and John, the men most closely associated with Him in His ministry, all testified that the Savior was God.

The authors of the first three Gospels also agree. Matthew names Him "Emmanuel . . . God with us" (Matt. 1:23). Mark opens his account with the words, "The beginning of the Gospel of Jesus Christ, the Son of God" (Mark 1:1). Luke calls the Lord Jesus, "The Holy One of God," "the Son of God."

Jesus' own cousin, John the Baptist, devoted his life to proclaiming that the one who would come after him was the Messiah. Pointing to Jesus Christ he cried, "I have seen and borne witness that this is the Son of God" (John 1:34).

In the Gospels you will find many other witnesses to His deity, such as Andrew, Philip, and Nathanael. The women who surrounded the Lord discerned His Godhead, and Martha and Mary worshipped at His feet.

The thief on the cross and the centurion in charge of His crucifixion both acknowledged that they were dealing with One who was outside the human sphere. "Truly this was the Son of God."

After the resurrection Thomas fell at His feet, crying, "My Lord and my God!" He was not rebuked by the Savior but gently chided because he had been so slow to comprehend the truth. Stephen, the

Ethiopian eunuch, Saul of Tarsus, men of the early church, proclaimed the truth of our Lord's deity.

Go through the history of the Christian church, and you will muster a vast army of those who believed that Jesus Christ is God. Apostles, fathers, martyrs, reformers, saints and faithful of all the centuries have bowed before the Lord Jesus and have acknowledged Him as the Son of God.

All the witnesses agree: He is God.

Now we turn from these witnesses and point out that the deity of the Lord Jesus Christ was affirmed by His resurrection.

I shall not take the space to present the evidence of the resurrection of Jesus Christ, except to say that there is proof sufficient for any open mind. If you refuse to believe that Jesus Christ rose from the dead, that is your choice. It is not because you cannot believe, for the facts are there. An unbeliever convinced against his will is of the same opinion still. In hell the rich man asked Abraham to send Lazarus back to earth to warn his brothers. When Abraham answered that they should read Moses and the prophets, the rich man argued that if one went to them from the dead they would repent. Abraham's answer shows the depths of sin in mankind: "If they hear not Moses and the prophets, neither will they be persuaded, though one rose from the dead" (Luke 16:29-31).

One of the mightiest proofs of the resurrection is the change of the day of worship from the Jewish Sabbath to the first day of the week, the Lord's Day. The astounding psychological change in the disciples can be accounted for only by the resurrection of Jesus Christ. They were transformed from cowards into indomitable men who feared neither life nor death, and that in the course of one day. It is totally impossible to explain these things apart from the historical, physical resurrection of Christ from the dead. Jesus rose from the dead in the same body in which He died. C. S. Lewis of Cambridge, in one of his notable books, discusses the theory that the resurrection was only spiritual, and he replies that the resurrection of Christ was as literal as broiled fish. The Lord Jesus appeared to His disciples beside the Sea of Galilee, broiled some fish for them, and ate with them. It was a real resurrection after a real death, the death of a man whose flesh had been pierced by a spear thrust into His side. He arose from the dead, and He lives today.

Our text now sets forth that His resurrection declares Him to be the Son of God with power, according to the Spirit of Holiness. The Bible presents three portraits of the Lord Jesus Christ. First, in the days of His flesh He is despised and rejected by men and put to death in shame and ignominy. Second, we see Him seated at the right hand of God in heaven, interceding for His church and furnishing power to His own to live victoriously in the world where He was crucified. Third, He is revealed as the coming Judge and Monarch who will put down sin and reign in righteousness. The resurrection is the vindication of Christ in His humility, the revelation of Christ in His present glory, and the guarantee of Christ in His coming power. Let us look at these three points more closely.

When Christ came, He put Himself into the hands of wicked men. He came into the world, the world which He had made, and the world knew Him not. He was despised and rejected by men, a Man of sorrows and acquainted with grief. Yet He declared that He was the Lord from heaven. He told His enemies that if they had known Him they would have known the Father also, and implied that because they did not know Him they could not know the Father. He said that He would leave them and that they would die in their sins, and that if they died in their sins they could never go where He went, because they believed not that He was Jehovah. When they quibbled with Him, He replied, "You are from below, I am from above; you are of this world, I am not of this world" (John 8:23).

He allowed Himself to be buffeted and spat upon. Was this the Son of God, the Lord Jehovah, the Word made flesh? They drove nails through His hands and feet; and when, after six hours, He dismissed His spirit, His lifeless body hung upon the cross until a soldier thrust a spear into His side. Was this the Son of God? They put Him into a tomb after wrapping His body in linen cloths like any other corpse. Was this the Son of God? The whole universe bent to see.

Then on the third day He brought light into that dark tomb. He took His body and left the cloth, like a chrysalis abandoned by a butterfly. He passed through the rocky walls of the tomb, alive forevermore. Then an angel rolled away the stone from the door, not to let the Lord Jesus out but to let the disciples in. He was not there. He had risen.

> *Death cannot keep his prey —*
> *Jesus, my Savior;*
> *He tore the bars away —*
> *Jesus, my Lord.*
>
> *Up from the grave He arose,*
> *With a mighty triumph o'er His foes.*
> *He arose a victor from the dark domain,*
> *And He lives forever with His saints to reign.*
> *He arose! He arose! Hallelujah! Christ arose!*

By that resurrection the meek and lowly Jesus was designated the Son of God with power. The Spirit of holiness had been upon Him throughout all His life, yet He died like a common thief. Was He a blasphemer, deserving of death? The resurrection vindicated Him and proved that He was what He declared Himself to be. Was this a mere man, born of natural human sperm? No! He lives, vindicated and enthroned in heaven, declared to be the Son of God by His resurrection from the dead.

The Bible's second picture of the Lord Jesus Christ shows Him as He is now, seated at the right hand of God in heaven, occupied with the high-priestly work of interceding for His own. His resurrection thus reveals Him to us. The unbeliever looks back to the historical Jesus and sees only a dim figure who once walked the earth and left a high code of ethics. But to the eye of the believer the Lord Jesus appears as the God of the universe, sharing the heavenly throne with His Father. In chapter 1 of the Book of the Revelation, John the evangelist on the isle of Patmos had a vision of the Lord in glory. It is a strange picture, if you try to visualize it, like a monstrosity in a believe-it-or-not column. John wrote: "I saw . . . one like unto the Son of man, clothed with a garment down to the foot, and girt about the breasts with a golden girdle. His head and his hairs were white like wool, as white as snow; and his eyes were as a flame of fire; and his feet like unto fine brass, as if they burned in a furnace; and his voice as the sound of many waters. And he had in his right hand seven stars: and out of his mouth went a sharp two-edged sword: and his countenance was as the sun shineth in his strength. And when I saw him, I fell at his feet as dead" (Rev. 1:12-17).

When traveling in Germany, I saw a painting in which the artist had attempted to depict this scene. A man dressed in white, with hair of white wool and feet of glowing brass, held seven stars in one hand. Out of His mouth came a tongue that was a two-edged sword, and two streaks of flame beamed from His eyes. It was a horrible picture. But God never meant that vision to be literal. Rather, it indicated what the resurrection had meant to the Lord Jesus Christ. If you have a good concordance, look up every detail and you will find parallels in the Old Testament. For example, where else in the Bible do we see someone with white hair? Turn to the Book of Daniel and read his description of the Lord God: "I beheld till the thrones were cast down, and the Ancient of days did sit, whose garment was white as snow, and the hair of his head like the pure wool . . ." (Dan. 7:9).

The Ancient of days whom Daniel saw was actually the Lord Jesus Christ enthroned in glory. Each detail of John's vision is an index reference to one of the great visions of the Old Testament. The Jesus whom the disciples saw ascend into heaven is the Lord Jehovah of Hosts, designated so with power by the resurrection from the dead.

It is thus that the Christian sees Him today. I never think of Jesus Christ as a figure of the past, or as a pain-distorted body on a crucifix. Oh, thank God, a believing Christian needs no crucifix! I do not worship a dead Savior; I worship the living, risen Christ. There He sits, yonder in the heavens, the guarantor of my faith and the surety for my salvation. When the winds of temptation blow hot, the risen Son of God with power makes intercession for me. When I stumble and fall, the risen Son of God with power restores me to grace and favor. For the force of the Greek word which says that He was declared to be the Son of God does not mean merely that He was *proclaimed* Son of God, but that He was *manifested* as the Son of God. His Godhead meets our every need and supplies us with unending blessings bought for us on the cross and guaranteed by the resurrection of the Lord Jesus Christ from the dead.

Is it any wonder that the believer celebrates Easter every day in the year? Do not limit us to one Sunday fixed by the moon in relation to the vernal equinox. Ecclesiastics have devised a calendar which allows Easter to dance along from March to April, but the child of God knows resurrection in the dead of winter or the heat of summer.

The resurrection of Jesus Christ has joined the believer to the risen Lord, and today, *today,* He lives. He lives on the throne of God, and He lives in the hearts of His redeemed.

In one way it would be pleasant to end our declaration here, but in faithfulness to the Word of God we must complete the story. The Bible tells us that the Lord Jesus Christ will return and judge this world. The madness of men runs its way of rejection. Jesus Christ is enthroned in the hearts of believers, but He is despised and rejected by the world. The fact that He has risen from the dead is God's pledge that He will come back and judge this accursed world. On Mars Hill, Paul reminded the people of Athens that all human beings are the offspring, the creatures of God, and are therefore responsible to Him. The Bible does not teach that all men are the children of God, but that all are the creatures of God. In order to be a child of God, you must be born again through faith in the finished work of Calvary.

Paul proclaimed, "We ought not to think that the Godhead is like unto gold, or silver, or stone, graven by art and man's device. And the times of this ignorance God winked at [overlooked]; but now commandeth all men everywhere to repent: because he hath appointed a day, in the which he will judge the world in righteousness by that man whom he hath ordained; whereof he hath given assurance unto all men, in that he hath raised him from the dead" (Acts 17:29-31).

This is the most solemn fact on record. It is the declaration that, if you do not flee to the cross and lay hold upon the redemption provided by the shedding of the blood of the Son of God, you will be judged by the Christ whom you have rejected. Human sin once turned the glory of Jehovah's Christ to shame. But now from heaven He shines, risen and exalted. And the day of His patience will end. He will lay aside His high-priestly garment and put on the sword of omnipotent justice. He was raised from the dead according to the spirit of holiness, and that holiness you will one day encounter. The resurrection is the pledge and guarantee that you will face the Lord Jesus Christ. You may think that you can stand before Him, but you cannot. If you are not robed in His righteousness provided through the atonement of the cross, you will appear before Him in the filthy rags of your own righteousness and He will send you to outer darkness forever.

This resurrection is a combination of power and holiness. Do not think that you can escape it. Holiness must be satisfied. God's power will reach you where you are, and silence your proud lips forever.

Jesus Christ has been declared the Son of God with power, according to the spirit of holiness by the resurrection from the dead. That resurrection is the vindication of His humility, the life and comfort of the believer, and the awful doom and despair of the unbeliever. Today is still the day of mercy and grace. The door of salvation stands wide open. Come to Him while it is yet day.

good chap

Chapter Three

IDENTIFIED WITH THE RISEN CHRIST

Have you ever stopped to think that one of the reasons the Lord Jesus Christ rose from the dead was that He might be your living, contemporary, your daily companion, your ever-present Lord? This was why He was raised from the dead by the glory of the Father (Rom. 6:4).

> *Christ the Lord is risen today, Alleluia!*
> *Sons of men and angels say; Alleluia!*
> *Raise your joys and triumphs high; Alleluia!*
> *Sing, ye heavens, and earth reply. Alleluia!*

Thus the church throughout our English-speaking world sings on the day of the resurrection. And thus we may sing today and every day. It makes no difference what Sunday of the year it may be: it is surely the day of the resurrection. Men of ritual and liturgy may divide the Sundays and call them Sundays in Trinity or Sundays in Advent; they may have special Sundays which they call Whitsunday or Nativity, but to the believer in the Lord Jesus Christ who comprehends spiritual truth each Sunday is the day

Easter hymns every Sun

of the resurrection. The songs which some churches sing only at Easter can and must be sung by us on any Sunday in the year. Yes! no matter what the day of the week may be, it is the day of the resurrection for the one who has been touched by the power of God and raised into the newness of that life of the resurrection along with the Lord Jesus. There is an old story of a minister who went to a country church in England to conduct the services for that day. When he entered the building before the hour of worship, he handed the verger a slip of paper with the numbers of the hymns to be posted on the announcement board. A few minutes later the verger tiptoed back into the vestry and asked whether a mistake had been made, for it was September and these hymns were for Easter. There was no mistake, and the people that day learned that resurrection day comes in any month of the year.

Christ was raised from the dead through the glory of the Father. The use of glory for the medium of the resurrection is most interesting. It is a simple figure of speech, a metonymy, where one word is used for another thing that it suggests. It is similar to Christ's words in the communion service, "As oft as you drink this cup." Anyone can understand that it is not the cup which is drunk, but the wine in the cup. And here we must understand that it was not the glory of the Father which raised Christ from the dead, but the power of God which performed such an amazing wonder that it was nothing short of glorious.

There is more to this than meets the eye at first glance. When we ask what was astonishing in this particular miracle, we are immediately drawn to consider the significance of the event and its implications. There were other resurrections beside the resurrection of the Lord Jesus, but none had so glorious a display of power. Elijah raised from the dead the son of the widow who had fed him during the years of famine. This was indeed a display of power, but there was no more to it than reversing the direction of an automobile. You bring your car to a halt, slip the gears easily into reverse, and back around to make a turn. The same principle was used by God on these other occasions to reverse the laws of decomposition and decay which were at work on a body which He determined to bring back to life. God, who had breathed the breath of life into the primal clay, could easily do it again after death had removed that breath from the body. Even when Christ raised bodies from the dead, He used only the simple power of His command.

But when the Lord Jesus Christ was raised from the dead, it was something far different. If we read all the passages in the Bible which refer to the resurrection of the Lord Jesus, we discover that the plan of God centered around it. This was the climax of the chain of events begun three days before when the Son of God was nailed to the cross as the Savior. He was not the Savior until then, and the resurrection was the declaration by the triune God that the plan of redemption had been fulfilled. Just as a diamond's many facets gather beams of light and reflect that light in flashing colors of prismatic glory, so the redemptive work of Christ and His resurrection catch the glory of God and display the wonders of His love and power.

When the son of the widow of Nain was raised from the dead, when the daughter of Jairus was commanded to arise at Jesus' command, when Lazarus was brought back to life, in each case only a single life was involved. But when the Lord Jesus Christ went to the cross, unnumbered millions of human beings were seen by God as on the cross with Him. Abel was there and all since Abel who have believed God's Word about the blood of the atonement. Enoch was there, and all who have walked with God crying out against the ungodliness of this present evil world. Noah was there, Abraham was there, and all who look for a city which has foundations, whose builder and maker is God. The infant child of David was there, and innumerable hosts of babies all over the world were there. Mary the mother of Jesus was there, for the original sin with which she was born was placed on that body of the Savior to which she had given birth. One of the two thieves who hung beside Him was seen by God as in Christ, and all like him who have trusted in the Savior were on Calvary with the dying Lamb.

I was there . . . that fact is the awe-inspiring wonder of my life. I contemplate it with an amazement that is indescribable. Why should He have loved me? But He did. When I was a young Christian I sang some of the great hymns without understanding what they meant. To be loved by Christ did not seem unusual; we

were not such unlovely people. But as the years went on, He taught
me the truth of such hymns as:

> *Beneath the cross of Jesus I fain would take my stand.*
> *or, Jesus, keep me near the cross.*
> *or, Alas! and did my Savior bleed, And did my Sovereign die?*

As I was drawn closer to the cross, the glory of Calvary really
took hold of me. While in my teens I sang in a duet a hymn whose
words were beautiful, but which now grip and stir me to the depths
of my soul as they never did in the days of my youth:

> *I stand all amazed at the love Jesus offers me,*
> *Confused at the grace which so freely He proffers me,*
> *I tremble to know that for me He was crucified,*
> *That for me, a sinner, He suffered, He bled and died.*
> *Oh! it is wonderful that He should care for me*
> *Enough to die for me! Oh! It is wonderful!*
> *Wonderful to me!*

Now, knowing that all believers were in Christ as He died, we
glimpse the amazing scope of the resurrection of the Lord Jesus
Christ from the dead. For He did not rise alone. That is the heart
of the gospel, the basic teaching of the Word of God. When He
arose from the dead, Abel, son of Adam and first to die upon this
earth, arose with Him. When He arose from the dead, Enoch,
though he was translated, received life evermore in the resurrection
of the Lord whom he loved and for whose return he looked. Noah
was there, vindicated forever by the triumph of the Lord who had
shut him into the ark and kept him through the flood. Abraham,
father of the faithful, arose, and all who have been blessed in the
covenant promises made jointly to him and to his seed, the Lord
Jesus Christ (Gal. 3:16). Yes, they were all there: David and
his infant child; the thief who believed on Him; His own mother,
Mary, forgiven and cleansed by the death of her Son; and all the
believers of all ages. And I was there. Over that fact I never
cease to marvel. No man who comprehends his identification with
Christ can be the same again.

This identification of all believers with the Lord Jesus in His

[handwritten margin note: That is: Such a fantastic display of power as to raise all who believe on that Easter morn.]

[handwritten margin note: We all died & arose in Him. That was His x Hes Ress. is so in A.]

death is what makes the resurrection so important. Because we are identified with the Lord Jesus, His resurrection called forth such a display of the power of God Almighty as to be described in terms of glory. In the epistle to the Ephesians, the Holy Spirit ransacked the vocabulary of power to describe the raising of our Lord from the dead. Paul prayed that the young believers might know "what is the exceeding greatness of his power to us-ward who believe, according to the working of his mighty power, which he wrought in Christ, when he raised him from the dead . . . and you . . . who were dead in trespasses and sins" (Eph. 1:19; 2:1). Strong though the passage is in English, the original Greek strikes hammer blows. The power which the Lord God displayed was indeed glorious.

In raising the Lord Jesus Christ from the dead the Lord God exhibited His power over sin, over death, over matter, over Satan, over time, over eternity.

By the resurrection of Jesus Christ the stroke of sin became ineffectual in destroying the sinner. Sin indeed brought physical death and the second death. But with the resurrection of the Lord Jesus Christ, the stroke of sin could no longer separate the sinner from God because the Lord Jesus had borne his sin. By coming to life through the glorious power of the Father, the Lord Jesus ended sin's dominion over the individual, even though Satan should attempt to shake that soul. Instead of sin, holiness would reign in the believer.

By the resurrection of the Lord Jesus Christ, death was rendered powerless. Like a scorpion, death had struck at man and its poison permeated all humanity. But when the glorious power of God was displayed and the life of the Lord once more swept through the tomb where they had laid His body, death lost its sting forever. Hear the cry of triumph: "O death, where is thy sting? O grave, where is thy victory?" (1 Cor. 15:55).

[handwritten margin note: 1 Cor 15 'Sting']

Likewise we see God displaying His glorious power over matter. He formed the body of man out of the dust of the ground, breathed into him the breath of life, and man became a living soul. Then Satan introduced sin, and death came to the race. The bodies of men grew old and declined and finally went into death and corruption. But of His own body Jesus Christ said, "Thou wilt not leave my soul in hell, neither wilt thou suffer thine Holy One to see corruption" (Acts 2:27). In the body of Jesus Christ, physical, tangible matter was different from all other matter on this planet. He could not be held by death (Acts 2:24); and thus, in His resurrection, He established the pattern for ours. These bodies of our humiliation will be made like His glorious body, by His power to subdue all things to Himself (Phil. 3:21). "So when this corruptible shall have put on incorruption, and this mortal shall have put on immortality, then shall be brought to pass the saying that is written, Death is swallowed up in victory" (1 Cor. 15:54). But the resurrection of the Lord Jesus has set the pattern for the victory to follow.

The glorious power displayed in bringing Him from the dead is the guarantee of the physical resurrection of all believers of all the ages, whose bodies have long since crumbled into dust. In the fields and seas of the world they lie — of whom the world was not worthy. There is the glorious company of apostles; the goodly fellowship of prophets; the noble army of martyrs; the holy Church. See them rise from the dead because He was raised from the dead by the glorious power of the Father. See the victims of the Inquisition and the martyrs of Scotland's hills. See them rise, like flowers thrusting up from the earth in springtime. Out of every cemetery in the world they come. Not one will be left behind. This dust of the human body will come forth from the grave in the triumph of resurrection life. This dust, this matter, the chariot of corruption and the vehicle of decay, will become a torch to blaze forever without being consumed, the chalice to hold the wine of eternal life.

The resurrection of the Lord Jesus Christ exhibited the power of God over the rebel Satan who thought that a will other than the will of God could maintain order in the universe. Satan had cried out, "I will ascend into heaven, I will exalt my throne above the stars of God: I will sit also on the mount of the congregation, in the sides of the north; I will ascend above the heights of the clouds; I will be like the most High" (Isa. 14:13, 14). But with the resurrection of Jesus Christ, the breath was taken from his boasting. He, who once knew the sweep of mighty angels in his train, shall be toppled into the lake of fire prepared for him and those angels who followed him (Matt. 25:41). Now the universe knows that no will but that of the God and Father of our Lord Jesus Christ can exist in the presence of the Prince of peace who has become the Lord of life.

The resurrection of the Lord Jesus Christ by the glorious power of the Father demonstrated also His lordship over time. In the midst of the ages the Savior died and rose again from the dead. Now our Lord could reach back to the garden of Eden and forward to the end of days and draw men to Himself. At the open tomb of the Lord Jesus, the ages telescoped into nothingness; time disappeared and forever lost its hold over the minds of those to whom God has given eternal life.

This victory will demonstrate the glorious power of our Lord throughout all eternity. The resurrection of Christ brought time and eternity together. Through the power of His resurrection we enter the timeless present; the past is blotted out by the blood of the Lord Jesus Christ, and the future flows in ecstasy without thought of time. This life is here and now for us who have believed on Jesus Christ. As believers, we live eternity in time. How can creatures of the time-world live outside its sphere? But how shall we, partakers of His glorious resurrection power, live any longer in time and for time? Eternity! Eternity! We enter into thee by the door of the resurrection of our Lord Jesus Christ; and having entered in, we want no more of this world. Henceforth our true home is in that eternal city which God has prepared for us.

Chapter Four

KNOWING THE RISEN CHRIST

The story of the resurrection of Jesus Christ has been told and retold for almost two thousand years; yet, like the sunrise, it is always new and fresh.

When we go back through the tomb to Christ's death, His life on earth takes on new significance. First, the sting of death is removed. When I was a small boy in California, my father kept bees, and one day I was stung. My mother heard me yell and came with a pair of tweezers. She pulled out the stinger and explained to me that when a honeybee stings someone, it loses its stinger and dies. On reading I Corinthians 15:55, "O death, where is thy sting?" I remembered that childhood incident and drew the spiritual parallel: Just as the bee stung my hand, then lost its sting and died, so Death stung the Lord Jesus and left scars in His hands — but the sting of death was removed and Death died! The Lord Jesus Christ died, but He rose again, conqueror over death! Paul writes, "Our Savior Christ Jesus . . . abolished death and brought life and immortality to light through the gospel" (2 Tim. 1:10).

Imagine a soldier alone in a foxhole on Guadalcanal. He hears the whine of a bullet, so he digs low and stays in his foxhole all day. As he seeks to dig a little deeper, water rises in the foxhole. He has nothing to eat but K rations, and for four days and nights he stays in that foxhole, fighting insects and living on K rations. He begins to appreciate how a horse feels when he eats only hay and oats, oats and hay. At the end of the fourth day someone comes and says, "Hey, are you Private Smith, No. 768-99-74?" "Well, what's it to you?" "I am to relieve you. You are to go behind the lines, get cleaned up, and put on a fresh uniform. You are getting a furlough back to the States, where you will sit at your mother's table and eat everything you like best." The soldier whines, "Must I leave this foxhole? Do you mean to say that I must leave Guadalcanal for home? Must I eat fried chicken instead of K rations?"

"What an impossible reaction!" you say. Yet when death approaches, many Christians cry, "Doctor, keep me alive three days more! I'll cash my insurance policy and pay it to you! Just keep me out of heaven three days longer." Since, however, "To depart and be with Christ is far better" (Phil. 1:23), perhaps such fearful Christians are not sure that they are going to heaven. When Charles Haddon Spurgeon was a young preacher, he wrote to the aged Horatius Bonar and asked for his picture. The old man sent it and wrote, "Dear Spurgeon: If you had waited a little, you could have had a better likeness, for soon I shall be like Him." Horatius Bonar understood that "though our outer nature is wasting away, our inner nature is being renewed every day" (2 Cor. 4:16). Christians can face death without fear because Jesus Christ is alive! A Moslem woman said to a missionary, "What did you do to my daughter?" The girl, sixteen years old, had died a few days before. The missionary, thinking that the mother was accusing him, replied, "Why, we didn't do anything to her!" But the woman said, "Yes you did! She died smiling, and our people don't die like that." How true! The Lord Jesus Christ by His resurrection has removed the terrors of death for those who put their trust in Him, and we die smiling. "O death, where is thy sting?" Since the Lord Jesus Christ died and rose again, death has no power over us.

But there is something even better than contemplating our joy and victory over death. Years ago, in the north of Ireland, a peddler called at a certain house. The householder said, "It's a grand thing to be saved!" The peddler replied, "Yes, but I know something better!" In astonishment the householder asked, "What could possibly be better?" And the answer was, "The companionship of the risen Christ; that is better even than salvation." To know I am saved, that I have eternal life, that I am not going to hell, yes, that is wonderful! But the companionship of the risen Christ is more wonderful. Oh, to know Him, to be with Him, to love Him!

If you speak foreign languages, you have doubtless used expressions in a foreign tongue without fully understanding their meaning. Likewise, a foreigner sometimes says things in English that he would never say in his mother tongue. Years ago, at Keswick, England, a German lady said to me, "You know, I know the Lord so well, we sometimes laugh together!" She probably would not have said that in her mother tongue! And it is not usual to say this in English. Nevertheless, that was what the Irish peddler meant when he said, "I know something better than being saved: it is the companionship of the risen Christ."

Oh, if you do not know the companionship of the risen Christ, then you have a low set of values! Are you more interested in watching television than in reading the Word of God and having fellowship with Him? Paul wrote: "I have suffered the loss of all things and count them as refuse, . . . that I may know him and the power of his resurrection, and may share his sufferings, becoming like him in his death" (Phil. 3:8,10).

When you know that Christ is risen, the orientation of life changes radically. A generation ago an Anglican bishop determined to go to China as a missionary. Someone said to him, "But Bishop, you will bury yourself in China!" He said, "Yes, I know, but I believe in the resurrection." It is a wonderful thing to be buried in China if God has sent you there, or to be buried in the work that God has given you to do at home. When you believe in the resurrection, all life takes on an entirely different hue. When you go back to the cross through the tomb, everything is changed. Jesus Christ said, "If any man would come after me, let him deny himself and take up his cross daily and follow me" (Luke 9:23). "Oh," says someone, "that is a burden!" When you know Christ in the power of His resurrection, to take up the cross is no more of a burden than wings are on a bird. Are wings a burden to a bird? Are the cross of Jesus Christ and companionship with Him burdensome? Of course not! "They who wait for the Lord shall renew their strength, they shall mount up with wings like eagles, they shall run and not be weary, they shall walk and not faint" (Isa. 40:31). God saved us not only to take us to heaven but to give us fellowship with Himself. God is more interested in you than you are in Him. God wants your companionship! He wants you close to Himself. Any father whose child has said, "Daddy, I love you!" has at least a dim idea of the joy that God the Father feels when a believer says, "Lord, You are more important than the job; You are greater than the disappointments and defeats. I love You and want to walk with You." Now the reason God saved us was that He loves Jesus Christ so much that He wants to duplicate Him in us. Did you ever stop to realize that Christianity actually is the duplication of Jesus Christ in you and me forever? "When he appears we shall be like him, for we shall see him as he is" (1 John 3:2).

When we believe on the Lord Jesus Christ, God begins to form Christ in us. This is the purpose of the resurrection. Jesus Christ rose from the dead that we might meet Him on some Damascus road as Paul did and that we might have Christ formed in us. Paul describes that purpose in Galatians: "He who had set me apart before I was born . . . was pleased to reveal his Son in me" (Gal. 1:15, 16). That is the great objective: God wants to reveal His Son in you.

This is why the Apostle Paul again and again in his letters calls to mind our position in the risen Lord Jesus. "I therefore, a prisoner for the Lord, beg you to lead a life worthy of the calling to which you have been called" (Eph. 4:1). Again, "I appeal to you therefore, brethren, by the mercies of God, to present your bodies as a living sacrifice, holy and acceptable to God, which is your spiritual worship. Do not be conformed to this world but be transformed by the renewal of your mind, that you may prove what is the will of God, what is good and acceptable and perfect" (Rom. 12:1, 2).

Paul realized that even in his day believers would be so engrossed in the things of the world that they would be asleep to their high privileges in Christ. He likens such a believer to a person who is so abnormal that he chooses to sleep in a funeral parlor among the corpses! This is the literal picture of Ephesians 5:14-16: " 'Awake, O sleeper, and arise from the dead, and Christ shall give you light.' Look carefully then how you walk, not as unwise men but as wise, making the most of the time, because the days are evil." The risen Lord Jesus Christ calls us to walk in Him among the spiritually dead of this world, not to lie down with them in sleep. So Paul continues, "If then you have been raised with Christ, seek the things that are above, where Christ is, seated at the right hand of God. Set your minds on things that are above, not on things that are on earth. For you have died, and your life is hid with Christ in God. When Christ who is our life appears, then you also will appear with him in glory" (Col. 3:1-4).

We may well pause and consider the expression, "where Christ is." Paul states that He is seated at the right hand of God. Have you ever stopped to think what that means? As I have said, we too often think of the Lord Jesus only as a historical figure, as having risen from the grave 1900 years ago. But have we recognized the fact that He is our contemporary; that He arose to be with us now; that we can have real, genuine fellowship with Him now; and that we are to meet Him at the throne of grace where He is seated with the Father? That throne of grace might well have been a throne of judgment to condemn us instead of a throne of grace to commend us! This is why Paul says, "Let us then with confidence draw near to the throne of grace, that we may receive mercy and find grace to help in time of need" (Heb. 4:16).

The question now occurs, "How can God reveal Christ in me?" God wants you to be conformed to the image of His Son in your school, office, hospital, store, factory, and, most important, in your family. But you may say, "I am nothing but a rough block of stone."

One of the greatest of American sculptors was Gutzon Borglum who died in 1941. He made the great carvings of the heads of Washington, Jefferson, Lincoln and Theodore Roosevelt on Mount Rushmore in South Dakota. At one time he worked for many months on a six-ton block of marble. A woman who cleaned his studio every day wondered what that great block was for. Finally, after much toil, the features began to emerge from the marble; when the cleaning woman saw them she exclaimed, "How did Mr. Borglum know that Abraham Lincoln was in that stone?" Oh, how did the Lord know that Jesus Christ could be seen in you and me, rough blocks that we are? He did! But believe me, that block of marble would still be only a block, were it not for the fact that Gutzon Borglum's mind and heart, and chisel and artisanship had worked upon it to form the colossal head of Lincoln which is now in the Capitol in Washington.

So we should say, "Lord, keep chiseling on me until someone recognizes that Christ lives in me." He loved us, He died for us, He rose from the dead, and He constantly works in order to form the image of Himself in us.

Thus, when we understand God's purpose in saving us, we shall gaze at the cross through the empty tomb and shall raise our eyes to heaven, where He sits at the right hand of God, making intercession for us until that day when He will come again, King of kings and Lord of lords. In deep humility we should surrender to Him, realizing the awful cost of His death that we might enjoy the intercession of His risen life. If there be sin in our lives, we should confess it, not because we must, but simply because we love Him and want no barrier between ourselves and Him.

> *When I survey the wondrous cross*
> *On which the Prince of Glory died,*
> *My richest gain I count but loss,*
> *And pour contempt on all my pride.*
>
> *Were the whole realm of nature mine,*
> *That were a present far too small;*
> *Love so amazing, so divine,*
> *Demands my soul, my life, my all.*

On that great day when He will come forth, King of kings and Lord of lords, He will lay aside the garments of His mediation and will put on the glorious robe of the conqueror. He will gird Himself with a sword, and the armies of heaven will follow Him. Then He will put His foot on this civilization of ours and all persons that offend His majesty, righteousness, and holiness. And out of this world He will carve a place of peace and joy, of justice and purity. When He accomplishes this, we shall sing, Hallelujah! "The kingdom of the world has become the kingdom of our Lord and of his Christ, and he shall reign forever and ever" (Rev. 11:15).

Chapter Five

THE GIFT OF THE RISEN CHRIST

Thus far, while standing on resurrection ground, we have beheld the glories of our risen Lord as we saw His cross through the open tomb. We have learned that by sovereign grace, through the new birth, we have been made members of the family of God. By the baptism of the Holy Spirit we have been made members of the church, the body of Christ (1 Cor. 12:13). Thus we are identified with our risen Lord, and day by day we may have personal fellowship with Him. Still the question may be gnawing at our hearts, "Why did the Savior die?" God's Word gives the answer, "If while we were enemies we were reconciled to God by the death of his Son, much more, now that we are reconciled, shall we be saved by his life" (Rom. 5:10). This verse assures us of Christ's divine power in our daily life since being saved through His life is much more than being reconciled to God. We now possess the power of Christ's resurrection.

We must carefully differentiate the different phases of the life of Christ. First, He eternally exists in the Father and represents us there in the eternal counsels of the Godhead. Then, in the fullness of time, God sent Him forth, "made of a woman, made under the law" (Gal. 4:4). For some thirty years He lived that second phase on earth. Third, He went to the cross and poured out that life for us. He thus satisfied God, laid the groundwork for our reconciliation and established the basis for righteous condemnation of the world.

The fourth phase of Christ's life followed His resurrection, when for forty days He manifested Himself. He held out His hands to be touched, and showed His side, into which Thomas was invited to thrust his hand. He appeared by the Sea of Galilee and ate broiled fish with the disciples, as though to demonstrate by the most commonplace act of life that His body was not a ghostly apparition but a real body of flesh and bones (Luke 24:39). Fifth, He ascended into heaven and the cloud of glory received Him out of sight (Acts 1:9). He took His place on the throne of heaven at the right hand of God the Father as our mediator and intercessor. In the future He will manifest the sixth phase of His life when He ceases His work of intercession and comes forth as Judge to put down all sin and unrighteousness forever. Seventh and last, He will finish His work of judgment, turn the kingdom over to the Father, and enter into the eternal phase of His life with us as His bride (1 Cor. 15:24, 28; Eph. 1:23).

I have set forth these seven phases of the life of Christ because some people assert that it was not necessary for Christ to shed His blood, since Romans 5:10 states that we are saved by His life. Such a conclusion is the conclusion of ignorance. Christ never taught salvation from sin through following the example of His earthly life. The idea that adopting a system of ethics could save a soul was everywhere denied by the Lord Jesus. He "came not to be ministered unto, but to minister, and to give his life a ransom for many" (Matt. 20:28). He came "to seek and to save that which was lost" (Luke 19:10).

There is an illustration of this truth in the Passover as established by God in Egypt. Each family of Israel secured a lamb, a firstling of the flock, and carefully examined it to make sure that it was without spot or blemish. The lamb was taken into the household on the tenth day of the month, kept there for three days, and killed

on the fourth day. Its blood was sprinkled on the two sideposts and
on the upper doorpost of the house (Ex. 12:7). Can you imagine
the scene in a family of Israel when the lamb was brought into the
house? If you have children, you know the excitement that attends
the bringing in of a fluffy chick or duckling at Easter time, so you
can visualize the effect of the bringing of a lamb into the house. We
may be sure that the children cuddled and petted the lamb, tied a
ribbon around its neck, and wondered at the warm life throbbing
beneath their touch. But the day came when it was necessary to
take that little lamb and kill it. Otherwise the oldest son in the
house would die under the stroke of the angel of death passing
over the land. The angel would be unmoved by the warmth or
beauty of the lamb. He would know that the shedding of the blood
of the lamb was an ugly thing. Death is always ugly. It is almost
as ugly as the sin that caused it. No plea would avail — the lamb
must die.

This is how it was when the Lord Jesus Christ was taken into
the house of Israel for three years. John the Baptist — John the
Identifier — looked over all the men of Israel and saw no one who
was without spot or blemish. But when the Holy Spirit led John
to Jesus Christ he cried out, "Behold the Lamb of God, which
taketh away the sin of the world" (John 1:29). Christ's outward
qualifications could pass, but God Himself declared that His Lamb
was also perfect within: "This is my beloved Son, in whom I am
well pleased" (Matt. 3:17). Thus the Lamb was taken into the
household of Israel. For three years after His baptism, Christ went
about doing good: He healed the brokenhearted and caused the
blind to see, the deaf to hear, and the lame to walk. He cleansed
the leper and raised the dead. He spake as never man spake. Was
this enough? Could this matchless life save anyone? The earthly
life of Jesus Christ could save no man. The Lamb must go to the
cross, shed His blood, and die. There must be payment to the
justice of God by the love of God. Satisfaction must be given to
God Himself. So the Lamb was put to death. There was no merit in
His life; there was life and health and peace in His death. All
blessings come from the Christ of Calvary.

Much more then, having been reconciled by the outpouring of His life in death, we shall be saved through the welling up of His life in resurrection. When we were dead He died for us; much more, having risen, He lives for us; much more, being reconciled we shall be kept saved through His being alive. This is why He said, "It is to your advantage that I go away" (John 16:7).

One day after Pentecost outbalances many days before Pentecost. Now there is a depth of salvation available for the believer which Abraham, Moses and David never knew, and which Peter, James and John did not know before the resurrection.

The advantage was bought and paid for by the death of Christ; the advantage is administered to us by the present life of Christ. Let me illustrate this by two stories. Many years ago I had a good friend who inherited a fortune from his father and conducted the family business. In the year 1929, shortly before the great depression, I was in his part of the United States and he took me for a drive in the country. We admired some of the panoramas from hilltops, and we talked of many things. Finally he said, "Donald, I have put you down in my will for ten thousand dollars. I have specified that it is not for your ministry, that you are to spend it upon yourself. The Lord has given me a great deal of money, while you are receiving only enough to get along nicely. I want you to know my regard for you, so I have put you in my will for this sum." I thanked him, and when I reached home I told my family about this coming legacy. I thought of a dozen ways to spend it! But I have never profited by that bequest — the man is not dead yet. I am delighted that he is still alive. I rather believe that his will has been changed, for he lost much in the depression, gave up the family estate and moved to narrower quarters, no longer as wealthy as when he made the bequest to me. This illustrates the Bible verse, "For where a will is involved, the death of the one who made it must be established. For a will takes effect only at death, since it is not in force as long as the one who made it is alive" (Heb. 9:16, 17). God has made a multitude of promises to us, but those promises were of no value until the Lord Jesus Christ died. His death made God's last will and testament available to us. Now the bequest is available. Christ has died; the testament is in force and the assets of God's estate are put down to our account.

There is another phase of this matter which can be illustrated by a second story. At the beginning of the depression there was a great scandal involving a certain man who had lived a most honorable life up to that time. He and his law partner had made considerable fortunes. In 1928 the partner died, leaving his friend as executor and administrator of the estate. Each month this man sent a large check to the widow. The will was probated and the estate began to be liquidated. For legal reasons, the assets of the estate were turned into cash and government bonds. Then came the great crash. The executor had, on margin, stocks that were selling at very high prices, and he had to put up more collateral. The market plummeted downward, and he mortgaged his home. Still the market fell, and so he pledged the securities of his friend to support his own holdings. A month later, there was no check for the widow and eventually the executor went to prison for his crime of misappropriation.

When the Lord Jesus Christ died, He left us a vast estate. But how would it be managed? Could our rights be dissipated? Could we lose our inheritance? Not with such a God as our God! Not with such a Savior as our Savior! On the third day, the Lord Jesus Christ rose from the dead and became the administrator of His own estate. He lives in order to take care of us for whom He died. Thus, since He died in order that all of the riches of God might be made available to us, much more can we be sure of our possessions because He arose from the dead in order to manage our affairs. That is exactly what He is doing today. He will never defraud us. He is the bridegroom, we are the bride and His banner over us is love. "If we believe not, yet he abideth faithful: he cannot deny himself" (2 Tim. 2:13).

Much more then, having become reconciled, we shall be kept safe by His resurrection life. His life for us and in us gives us strong confidence and sustains our hope of present triumph and future oneness with Himself forever.

Let us look at the fact that we have been joined to Christ in His resurrection. He said, "Because I live, ye shall live also" (John 14:19). In the epistles this statement is expanded to reveal a prospect of life in Christ that one could never imagine. The tragedy is that few professing Christians enter into possession of that life. For the Lord was not talking about life in heaven after we die but the life of triumph on earth after we are saved.

On the day of Pentecost, Peter set forth the facts concerning the death and resurrection of Christ with His present position and power toward us: "This Jesus God raised up, and of that we all are witnesses. Being therefore exalted at the right hand of God, and having received from the Father the promise of the Holy Spirit, he has poured out this which you see and hear" (Acts 2:32, 33). In the eighth chapter of Romans this was carried one step further: "Who is he that condemneth? It is Christ that died, yea rather, that is risen again, who is even at the right hand of God, who also maketh intercession for us" (Rom. 8:34).

> The Father hears Him pray,
>   His dear anointed One;
> He cannot turn away
>   The presence of His Son.
> The Spirit answers to the blood
>   And tells me I am born of God.

In His intercession for us, Christ does more than remind the Father that we have been justified and that our sins have been dealt with forever. He takes us to the heights of God's purpose for us if we will surrender to the working of His power and recognize the possibilities of our oneness with Him. That theme is more briefly mentioned in the epistle to the Hebrews where we read, "Wherefore he is able also to save them to the uttermost that come unto God by him, seeing he ever liveth to make intercession for them" (Heb. 7:25). To be saved to the uttermost is the plan of God for us. When I was a boy, I memorized this verse as though it read that He is able to save us *from* the uttermost. I thought of the drunkards around town and imagined that this meant that God was able to stoop lower than anything I had known. A few years later, I heard Mel Trotter, the famous mission worker, tell the story of his life. He closed the account thus: "God saved me from the guttermost to the uttermost." I checked in my Bible and discovered that the text did, indeed, teach that God was able to save *to* the uttermost. Salvation for our present existence is a superlative possibility, but few Christians know it. If you can catch a vision of the meaning of our text — "much more shall we be saved by his life" — you may enter into that *much more* salvation which is available at the present time.

When the Lord Jesus Christ was here on earth, He stretched the chain of power from heaven direct to us for daily appropriation. In the Psalms we read, "God hath spoken once; twice have I heard this; that power belongeth unto God" (Ps. 62:11). That is wonderful to contemplate. Knowing that the source of all power is in God, we can rest quietly in the midst of a world where wickedness is apparently victorious. Paul wrote: "There is no power but of God: the powers that be are ordained of God" (Rom. 13:1). But the Lord Jesus after His resurrection boldly stated, "All power is given unto me in heaven and in earth" (Matt. 28:18). Today God the Father does everything through God the Son. The Lord Jesus is the repository of all the power in the universe. There is no power except His.

But what does Christ choose to do with all that mighty depot of power that is lodged in Him since the resurrection? The very last words which He ever spoke while on earth were these: "But ye shall receive power, after that the Holy Ghost is come upon you: and ye shall be witnesses unto me" (Acts 1:8); beginning with where you are, extending to the territory round about you and the territory a little farther off, and even unto the uttermost parts of the earth. The power inherent in God was transmitted to Christ in His resurrection and made available by Him to us before His ascension. This is why Paul cried out, "That I may know him, and the power of his resurrection" (Phil. 3:10). And having learned some of the lessons, he wrote to the Philippians in the next chapter, "I can do all things through Christ which strengtheneth me" (Phil. 4:13).

The channel of power has been fully prepared. It runs from the heart of God through the Lord Jesus Christ, flows down upon us from the cross and floods the open tomb. It carries us even to the throne of God, where we have been raised to sit together in the heavenly places in Christ (Eph. 2:6). O mighty flow of love! O blessed flow of grace! May we ever ride its crest, be carried beyond the rocky trials of this life and rest in the heart of God through our Lord Jesus Christ. Much more! Much more! We shall ever be kept safe in His life.

PART TWO

THE PERSON OF THE LIVING CHRIST
"That I May Know Him"

Because we have been made partakers of the divine nature, it is our great responsibility to know the person of our risen Lord in our daily lives, in order that we may have Him walking with us in all of life's situations.

Christology

Chapter Six

OUR UNIQUE CHRIST

Every Sunday-school child in France early learns the verse that is taught in Sunday schools the world over. French children recite John 3:16 like this: "*Car Dieu a tant aimé le monde qu'il a donné son Fils unique . . . .*" "God so loved the world that he gave his *unique* Son." One dictionary defines *unique* as "without like or equal." Another renders it, "the only one of its kind." Still another says, "single in kind or excellence; matchless." Now all these definitions may be applied to our Lord Jesus Christ. God gave His unique Son — matchless, without like or equal, the only one of His kind. He is the Lord of glory. Let us see in what ways the Lord Jesus Christ was unique.

use Jn 3:16

First, the Lord Jesus Christ was unique in His origin. The history of every other human being begins at birth: but the Lord Jesus Christ exists eternally as the Second Person of the Godhead. Before He was born at Bethlehem, He lived; He was one with the Father in essence and being. Before He came to earth as a baby, He walked among men and revealed Himself to them. The Old Testament, which was completed four centuries before His birth, contains

1.

many stories of His appearing among men before He came as babe, child and man.   He said, "Abraham rejoiced to see my day: he saw it, and was glad."   When the Jews protested, Jesus answered, "Verily, verily, I say unto you, Before Abraham was, I am (John 8:56, 58).   The appearances of God in the Old Testament cannot be explained apart from the fact that it was the Lord Jesus Christ making Himself known to the sons of men in connection with the call and keeping of Israel and in preparation for His coming.

In the Book of Isaiah we have a vision of the Lord God of Hosts, and we hear the seraphim cry out, "The whole earth is full of his glory" (Isa. 6:1-3).   In the New Testament John quotes from Isaiah 6 and says, "These things said Esaias, when he saw his glory, and spake of him (John 12:41).   Things equal to the same thing are equal to each other.   The Jesus of the fourth Gospel is none other than the Lord God of Hosts seen by Isaiah.

In the Book of Daniel, when the three Hebrews were thrown into the fiery furnace because they refused to worship the golden image, King Nebuchadnezzar peered into the furnace and cried out in astonishment, "I see four men loose, walking in the midst of the fire . . . and the form of the fourth is like the Son of God" (Dan. 3:25).   In the New Testament we get the explanation: "Have this mind among yourselves, which you have in Christ Jesus, who, though he was in the form of God, did not count equality with God a thing to be grasped, but emptied himself, taking the form of a servant, being born in the likeness of men" (Phil. 2:5-7).   He was indeed unique in His origin.

Second, the Lord Jesus Christ was unique in His birth.

There can be no doubt that the Bible teaches that Jesus was born without a human father.   So-called theologians have said that the doctrine of the virgin birth is not important; but if Christ's birth were not unique, the Bible would have no authority; there would be no assurance about any phase of His life, teaching, example, death, resurrection and return.   If Christ had not been born supernaturally without a human father, His nature would be that of the ordinary human being.   He would be a child of Adam, in whom all die; a sinner like all other men, and so unable to be the Savior of the human race.   He would Himself have needed a Savior, even as the Virgin Mary needed Him to be *her* Savior. She recognized this fact, for she sang in the Magnificat, "My soul magnifies the Lord, and my spirit rejoices in God my Savior" (Luke 1:46). But since Jesus Christ had the divine nature of God His father, He was indeed the sinless Son of God.

During Jesus' childhood it was quite natural that Mary's husband Joseph should be called the father — the accepted form of address used by adopted or stepchildren. At the age of twelve, Jesus stayed behind in Jerusalem when His parents started back to Nazareth. After an anxious search, they found Him in the temple. Chiding Him in the same terms as for her other children — Jesus' half-brothers and sisters — Mary said, "Son, why have you treated us so? Behold your father and I have been looking for you anxiously!"

With great gentleness our Lord rebuked her, and she must have gasped at the thought that she had allowed their relationship to crowd out the memory of His unique birth: "How is it that you sought me?" Jesus asked. "Did you not know that I must be in my father's house?" (Luke 2:48, 49). The fact that Mary and Joseph did not understand this reply in no wise lessens the strength of Christ's statement that Joseph was not his real father.

Third, the Lord Jesus Christ was unique in His being.

Christ's essential nature is that of holiness and love. History has focused on Him as on no other man. Those who trust Him as Savior and Lord have studied every word and gesture, analyzed His motives, watched His actions, appraised His message. Even more closely have His enemies scrutinized Him. Friend or foe, every man must consider Him. Jesus asked His opponents, "What do you think of the Christ? Whose son is he?" (Matt. 22:42). And His enemies have been forced to endorse the verdict of Pilate: "I find no fault in him" (John 19:4). They refuse to worship Him, not because they find fault in Him, but because they allege that Christ's followers claim for Him what, they say, He does not claim for Himself. When you ask by what authority they distort the Gospel narratives, they can only answer, "Well, it just stands to reason that. . . ."

Furthermore, attacks on His followers and on the veracity of the Word are rendered futile time and again. For example, during the first half of the twentieth century scientific theological journals asserted that the Gospel of John was not written until two hundred years after Christ. Then archaeologists discovered the mummy of a man, the date of whose death was known to be about A.D. 100. In the wrapping was a large fragment of papyrus containing part of the Gospel of John. The record stands. The Lord Jesus is unique in His being: He is the God of glory.

Fourth, the Lord Jesus Christ was unique in His doctrine.

"I am the truth!" He declared (John 14:6). His words alone have stood the test of history without being refuted.

When He was here on earth the Pharisees hated Him and sent soldiers to arrest Him. They came back without any prisoner, and to the consternation of the authorities these soldiers were completely convinced by Him. "No man ever spoke like this man!" (John 7:46) was all that they could say to account for their failure to complete their mission. The Lord Jesus pointed to the Old Testament, established its authority as divine (Mark 7:7-13), and asserted that it was all written about Him (Luke 4:21; John 5:45-47). No other man who ever lived and taught dared to say that supernatural knowledge would be given to any and every follower who would make a simple test: but Jesus did, for He said, "If any man determines to do God's will he shall know whether the teaching is from God or whether I am speaking on my authority" (John 7:17).

His teaching encompassed the past and the present need of men; it embraced the throne of heaven and the future of the ages; and He made Himself the center of it all. Whether He spoke comfort to the sorrowing, consolation to the bereaved, strength to the weak, courage to the fearful and judgment to the hardhearted, His words took on the flash and power of eternity. There is but one answer to the question, "Who is the greatest teacher of all time?" Even those who refuse to acknowledge Him as God still accept His teachings as the goal toward which men should work. Jesus Christ was absolutely unique in His doctrine and in all His words.

Fifth, Jesus Christ was unique in all that He did.

He met many sick people, but He never left a man in sickness. There were many blind people, but once they met Him they were blind no longer. He cast out demons from every oppressed person whom He met, and He broke up every funeral procession that crossed His path. Frequently He stood alone before His enemies; yet they feared Him. He made a whip of cords and, single-handed, overturned the tables of the moneychangers and drove them from the temple. He took the four seasons in His fingers: produced grain that was harvested, winnowed, ground into flour, baked into bread for a small boy's lunch, and gave that bread to the multitudes to eat. He walked upon the sea, and once when He lay asleep in the stern of the disciples' boat, they awakened Him, crying out that they were perishing in the midst of a storm. Calmly He arose and quelled the angry waters with a word that is ordinarily used to order a dog to lie down. Certainly our Lord was unique in all that He did.

Sixth, the Lord Jesus was unique in His death.

In the Garden of Gethsemane, the Lord Jesus was surrounded by a large company of soldiers who came with clubs and swords to arrest Him. Calmly He stood before them and asked, "Whom do you seek?" When they answered, "Jesus of Nazareth," He replied, "I AM" (John 18:5). This was the name which God used when speaking to Moses at the burning bush: "Say this to the people of Israel, 'I AM has sent me to you,'" (Exod. 3:14). When Jesus announced His deity in the garden, that large body of men "drew back and fell to the ground," and only at His will and by His permission did they rise to seize and bind Him. When He was brought before Herod He spoke not a word. While on the cross He maintained complete control of the situation. Through the hours of dying He spoke clearly and distinctly. This Man, the Lord of Glory, had said, "I am the Life"; and it is impossible to put Life to death. He did not bow His head until the final moment (John 19:30). Far from ending His suffering with mumbling whispers, He was strong to the last and "cried with a loud voice . . . , 'Father, into thy hands I commend my spirit'" (Luke 23:46). Had there been a physician attending the death of Christ, he could have given but one answer to the inquiry, "Cause of death?" It was certainly not from the multiple wounds and lacerations which he had received from those who had scourged Him and the soldiers who had buffeted Him; it was not from the loss of blood, although all had drained from His body.

He died because "He dismissed His spirit." That was the cause of death. Earlier He had said, "No man takes my life from me: I lay it down of my own accord. I have power to lay it down, and I have power to take it again" (John 10:18).

His death was also unique because it was planned by His heavenly Father. To understand the death of Christ, we must realize that He was put to death by God the Father. "It pleased the Lord to bruise him; he hath put him to grief" (Isa. 53:10). This prophecy concerned the purpose of His death, and this was the explanation that was given on the day of Pentecost when the doors were opened for men to come to God through the Lord Jesus Christ.

In Acts 2:22, 23, Peter announced: "Jesus of Nazareth, a man attested to you by God with mighty works and wonders and signs which God did through him in your midst, as you yourselves know — this Jesus, delivered up according to the definite plan and foreknowledge of God, you crucified and killed by the hands of lawless men."

Everywhere the Bible maintains the theme that His death was on behalf of sinners. He died for others. He died for the ungodly. He died for me. He died for you, whoever and wherever you are. He took all our sin upon Himself at Calvary. Thus, His death was unique.

Seventh, the Lord Jesus Christ was unique in His resurrection. The tomb of Mohammed lies at Mecca. The tomb of Confucius is in a cave on a sacred hill in China. But we must turn to the Lord Jesus Christ alone and proclaim, "He lives!" In both the Old and the New Testament, people were raised from the dead, but they lived to die again. This Man — the Lord Jesus Christ — died and lives again to die no more. Listen to Peter on the day of Pentecost: "But God raised him up, having loosed the pangs of death, because it was not possible for him to be held by it" (Acts 2:24). How I love that verse! I can almost feel Peter trembling with joy as he proclaimed before men, angels and demons: "It was not possible for Christ to be held by death!"

Now let us sum up all the ways in which our Lord Jesus Christ was unique: He was unique in His origin, for He came from the throne of God. He was unique in His birth, for He was born of a virgin without a human father. He was unique in His being, for no man has ever found a fault or flaw in Him. He was unique in His doctrine, for He made Himself the center of all Bible teaching. He was unique in His works, for sickness and death, storm and fury, could not stand before Him. He was unique in His death, for He controlled the entire situation and dismissed His spirit. He was unique in rising from the dead. Is it any wonder that He is unique in what He can do for you? This is absolute truth, for there is no human need that cannot be met by the Lord Jesus Christ.

Do you need Him to deal with your past? He is the only one who can blot out your sins. Since you have trusted in Him as your Savior, your sins have been cast behind His back (Isa. 38:17); cast into the depth of the sea (Micah 7:19); removed as far as the east is from the west (Ps. 103:12); remembered against you no more (Jer. 31:34).

Do you need Him to deal with your present life? He does not save you *in* your sins but *from* your sins (Matt. 1:21). He has promised that sin shall not have dominion over you (Rom. 6:14). He has promised to furnish you with pardon, peace, purity, power, hope, heaven, Himself. "How shall he not with him also freely give us all things?" (Rom. 8:32). There is no denying these promises. They bind us to Christ and unite us with Him. We can no more get out of Christ than Christ can get out of the Father, "For . . . your life is hid with Christ in God" (Col. 3:3). We are complete in Him (Col. 2:10). We are safe in Him; we are secured in Him. We may be constantly filled with joy in Him.

Do you need Him to plan your future? Our future is as bright as the promises of God. His Word cannot fail, and He has said that He will bring us all to the Father's house. He assures us of entrance into the home of God, and we shall be the fullness of Him who fills all in all. "It does not yet appear what we shall be, but we know that when he appears we shall be like him, for we shall see him as he is" (1 John 3:2).

Surely our Christ is unique! There is none like unto Thee, O Lord!

He "I am"

Chapter Seven

THE INDISPENSABLE CHRIST

In the preceding study we saw the uniqueness of our Lord Jesus Christ. Now we shall see that He is not only unique, but He is also indispensable. To His disciples He said, "Without me you can do nothing" (John 15:5).

Many Christians know this verse by heart but live as though Christ had said, "Without Me you can't do very much." Sometimes we hold the idea that God had better bless our plans, because if He doesn't, we are determined to go ahead with them anyhow. What I am saying is that many believers in Christ have not understood the ways of God. Our Lord did not say, "Without Me you can't do very much," but "Without Me you can do *nothing*." It is so flat and definite a statement that often it does not have the effect on us that it should have. We live in a world where we have to do things for ourselves. Our mothers and fathers spend months on us as babies and cheer our every progress. Putting a spoonful of food into the mouth without dripping is a major triumph. Buttoning a button is an event to be inscribed in the baby book. Standing up and walking alone is a heroic wonder to be remembered and cited even unto the second generation.

At the same time that we are learning that it is good and desirable to be able to do things without the help of others, we are supposed to learn that without the Lord we can do nothing. Some people never learn the lesson of this paradox.

Some people must be sent to outer darkness, separated from God forever, because they will not learn that they cannot save themselves: they must cease from their own works, as God did from His, and enter into the rest that is offered in Jesus Christ (Heb. 4:10). Some believers in Christ will see all their works burned away and themselves saved, but as by fire (1 Cor. 3:15), because they have not learned to cease from their own strength and efforts in doing the work that God has given them to do.

Physically, mentally and spiritually, we are dependent upon our God. He is indispensable in every phase of life. He maintains and sustains life, both here and on the other side of death.

First of all, He says, "I am the life." It should be self-evident that we cannot live without the Lord. We are creatures who can draw only one noseful of air at a time. We draw it in, full of life-giving oxygen, and we send it out carbon dioxide, which will kill any life that tries to live in its concentration. If a man puts a plastic bag around his head and ties it tightly to his neck, he will die of his own breath in a few moments. No atheist can cry his atheism twice without getting air from God in order to do it. He breathes in deeply and says, "There is no God," and then his lungs are emptied, and he cannot say it again until God lets him refill his lungs. The same is true for everything in life. I cannot say, "God is love," until He gives me the air to say it.

The Lord Jesus said, "A man can receive nothing, except it be given him from heaven" (John 3:27). This sentence can be pushed to the utmost extremity of thought, "For in him we live, and move, and have our being" (Acts 17:28).

We are dependent upon the Lord in every living second of our life, and when death comes we are dependent upon Him to bring us into heaven.

Second, He says, "I am the bread of life." This can be taken in two ways. He gives us all that we need for our food. To the Oriental this would have to be translated, "I am the rice of life," and to the inhabitant of a tropical isle, "I am the fish and bananas of life." He makes the sun to rise and the rain to fall. He who imprisoned the life germ in the grain of wheat or rice is the one who can make it germinate and come forth a hundredfold to give seed to the sower and food to the eater.

But in quite another way He is the one who gives us spiritual bread for our spiritual need. Christ said, "Man shall not live by bread alone, but by every word that proceeds from the mouth of God" (Matt. 4:4). We have the physical nature that must be nurtured with physical food and we have the spiritual nature that must be nurtured with spiritual food. In the unregenerate man that spiritual nature is carnal, fleshly, and is nourished by all the stimulants of a civilization that exists and profits on the needs of the physical, sexual, animal nature of man, on the prides and the passions with which our first nature is overstocked. In the regenerate man there is a new nature, a truly spiritual nature, which must be nourished by the Word of God. It is impossible for any Christian to maintain a spiritual life apart from the study and nourishment that God has given us. The Holy Spirit has urged: "As newborn babes, desire the sincere milk of the word, that ye may grow thereby" (1 Pet. 2:2). "Yes, without Me," says Christ, "without Me as bread you can do nothing."

Third, Jesus Christ said, "I am the light of the world" (John 8:12). There is much taught in the Bible concerning light. We now know much about light that our forefathers never dreamed of. They knew only the white light that is separated into the colors of the rainbow; but today we know that there is a light below red and beyond violet — infra-red and ultra-violet. We can talk of cosmic rays, alpha, beta, gamma rays, X-rays, and many others. But the Word of God says, "This is the message we have heard from him and proclaim to you, that God is light and in him is no darkness at all" (1 John 1:5).

When sin entered the universe, darkness came with it. Between verses 1 and 2 of Genesis 1 we can allow space for all that the Bible reveals elsewhere about the fall of Lucifer who became Satan

(Isa. 14:12-15). When he fell, sin entered the universe and brought the darkness of God's judgment. "The earth became a wreck and a ruin, and darkness was upon the face of the deep" (Gen. 1:2). Yet through Isaiah God tells us that He did not create the earth a chaos (Isa. 45:18).

Friends have tried to persuade me that the theory of a "gap" between the first two verses of Genesis is "unscholarly." I shall willingly abandon this idea if they can find another place before Genesis 3:1 to which we can consign the fall of Lucifer and the origin of sin. To date they have not found an alternate place.

The darkness which surrounded the early creation like a shroud fell also over the much later creation after man lost the image of God. Christ the light came into that darkness, which could not perceive Him because of the evil deeds of mankind (John 1:4,5). He enlightens every man who comes into the world; but men react to His presence like worms and slugs which are exposed to light when a board is turned over. They flee to darkness because they are afraid to face the light of His holy presence.

How do we become believers in Christ? Paul tells us: "It is the God who said, 'Let light shine out of darkness,' who has shone in our hearts to give the light of the knowledge of the glory of God in the face of Christ" (2 Cor. 4:6).

Fourth, we hear Christ saying, "I am the way" (John 14:6). How do we know which way to turn in all the bewildering choices of life? How shall we find the right path? When we believe on Christ as Savior, we learn that He is God's way. Anywhere He leads is the right path, and where He does not lead is the wrong one. Without Him there is no direction to life. The unsaved man needs Christ as the only way of salvation; the believer needs Him as the indispensable way of daily life.

How can a believer be sure that he is walking in God's way? First, the will of God always agrees with the Word of God. Second, the believer must surrender to God's will before he knows what it is. Third, if the first two conditions are met, God guarantees that He will reveal the way in which He wants His child to go: "Your ears shall hear a word behind you saying, 'This is the way, walk in it'" (Isa. 30:21). Christ goes before; if we are yielded to Him, it is impossible to make a mistake. Following Him, we know we are right. He who said, "Without me you can do nothing," has also said, "I am the way"; without Him as the way, we can know nothing.

In the fifth place, Christ has said, "I am the truth." Without Him we shall always be in error and ignorance. Wherever we seek for truth, we shall always find that the ultimate source is Christ. What is the truth about God? There is only one God, the God and Father of our Lord Jesus Christ. What is the truth about man? How can man truly know himself? No man ever knows himself until he understands that Christ had to die to redeem him, so low had he fallen in sin. Only in finding Christ the Truth can man really know himself.

What is the truth about the past? Only Christ can draw back the veil and reveal to us a past more ancient than creation. He was in the beginning with God because He was and is God. "All things were made by him; and without him was not anything made that was made (John 1:1-3). What about the future? Christ the Truth tells us that the hour will come when all who are in the grave will hear His voice and shall come forth to the judgment which God the Father has committed to Jesus Christ who is God the Son (John 5:22). The issues of eternity are settled in this life. All who reject Christ are eternally separated from God; all who receive Him possess life eternal. Thus, without Christ the Truth, we dwell in eternal ignorance, for without Him we can know nothing.

In the sixth place, Christ said, "I am the true vine" (John 15:1). Just outside London, in Hampton Court, is one of the largest grapevines in the world. The root stock is larger than many a tree, and the branches run as far as one hundred feet from the main stem. This one vine produces a prodigious quantity of grapes. However, even the smallest and remotest twig draws its life and productive power from the vine to which it is attached. The Lord used this simple fact to illustrate that He alone has life, and we can produce no lasting service except by His vital power operating in and through us. We win other men from darkness to light only because we are joined to the Vine and allow His life to flow through us.

In the seventh place, Christ tells us that He is the Good Shepherd (John 10:11, 14). In this image He presents Himself as the one

who protects us from the wolves of life, who leads us through green
pastures and beside still waters. The shepherd feeds, protects, nurses
and cares for his flock. Christ the Good Shepherd proved His
goodness and love by laying down His life for the sheep — the
one animal that cannot exist without a shepherd. In the spiritual
realm, without Christ the Shepherd we cannot live or do anything.
"Without me you can do nothing."

In the eighth place, Christ is indispensable because He is the door,
by whom, "if any man enter in, he shall be saved, and shall go in
and out, and find pasture (John 10:9). Thus He tells us that we
may freely come to Him, draw the breath of life and go out to exhale in activity for Him; then go in again and begin a new cycle.
When Christ called Himself the Shepherd, He united to it the
statement that He is the door of the sheepfold, and He warned against
hirelings and false shepherds. Remember His warning, and turn
away from anyone who would point you to some door other than
Christ, some shepherd who is not the Lord. Turn from anyone who
claims to possess the keys to the door that is wide open or makes
any other claim that detracts from the only Shepherd.

John 15:5 not only tells us that without Christ we can do nothing,
but it also tells us that, having Him, we have all that is
necessary. In the gospel story one of the most important words
is *alone*. Some who say that they believe in Christ will not
declare faith in Him *alone*. He is the open door, and there is no
other door into the kingdom of heaven. Without Him we can do
nothing; with Him we can do all things (Phil. 4:13).

In the ninth and last place, Christ says, "I am the resurrection,
and the life (John 11:25). Ever since Adam and Eve beheld the
lifeless body of their murdered son Abel, there has been a mystery
about death; men fear death as children fear the dark. When the
Lord Jesus rose from the dead, He dispelled that mystery and that
fear. When the stone was rolled away from the door to reveal that
the Lord had arisen, that He was alive, death lost its terror. For
those who are in Jesus Christ, death is but a door from the dark
tomb to a sunlit garden. We follow the coffin of a loved one to
the graveyard and, like the four men who took the palsied man to
the roof, we let the body down out of sight; but the soul is in the

presence of the Lord Jesus Christ. We know that our loss is only temporary, that we shall be reunited on the other side of the grave (1 Thess. 4:13-18).

When in John 14:6 Christ said, "I am the life," He meant the life which we receive when we are born again. But in John 11:25 He is referring to the life beyond the grave; there we shall see Him and be like Him, when we see Him as He is. Without Him, the resurrection and the life, we shall never know eternal life.

Oh, praise God for our indispensable Lord Jesus Christ! Without Him we can do nothing, for He has said, "I am the life; I am the living bread; I am the light of the world; I am the way; I am the truth; I am the true vine; I am the good shepherd; I am the door; I am the resurrection and the life."

How truly, how finally He spoke when He said, "Without me you can do nothing."

Chapter Eight

Sonship

THE SURRENDERED CHRIST

Why did Christ die? And why did Christ rise again? There are two different ways of looking at it: one from the standpoint of the Savior Himself, and one from the standpoint of God the Father. These two views are presented in the Scripture for a distinct purpose.

We believe without question that Jesus Christ is God, the second person of the Trinity, and that He eternally exists in that oneness and equality with the Father which is set forth throughout the Scriptures. But because our Lord Jesus loved us so much, He voluntarily subordinated Himself in the Incarnation; and in one sense that subordination to the Father will last through all eternity.

Our Lord made definite declarations about His own relationship to His death and His resurrection. He spoke one day to the people saying, "I am the good shepherd, and know my sheep, and am known of mine. As the Father knoweth me, even so know I the Father: and I lay down my life for the sheep. . . . Therefore doth my Father love me, because I lay down my life, that I might take it again. No man taketh it from me, but I lay it down of myself.

I have power to lay it down, and I have power to take it again. This commandment have I received of my Father" (John 10:14-18).

In order to understand this, it is necessary to go into the councils of eternity and listen to the Father and Son speaking together. It is possible to reconstruct the conversation because of certain phrases in various parts of the Bible. When it was determined that there should be a creation and that man should be given a free will, God knew, of course, that man would turn that free will to himself, and thereby bring the condemnation of God upon him. It would be necessary for the God of all holiness and all justice to strike with perfect wrath against the sinner. But the Godhead, Father, Son and Holy Spirit, decided that the Son should become a man and be perfectly obedient to the Father in everything, and that He should voluntarily submit to the stroke of that divine wrath, placing Himself in a position where God the Father would have to strike Him to death. The Son announced that He would do this, and thus He became the Lamb, slain from the foundation of the world (Rev. 13:8). At the time of the Incarnation we read, "Wherefore, when he cometh into the world, he saith, Sacrifice and offering thou wouldest not, but a body hast thou prepared me: In burnt offerings and sacrifices for sin thou hast had no pleasure. Then said I, Lo, I come (in the volume of the book it is written of me,) to do thy will, O God" (Heb. 10:5-7).

It is absolutely impossible to understand Christianity unless we realize that God the Father put Jesus to death on the cross. It is theological ignorance to emphasize that the Jews delivered Him to the secular arm of the Roman power and to blame the Jews as a race. The fact that Jewish officials delivered Christ to the Gentiles for crucifixion is relatively unimportant. Nor am I teaching that the fault lay with the Romans who actually drove the nails into the hands and feet of Christ. Again, this is relatively unimportant. Christ said, "No man taketh my life from me; I lay it down of myself." No one could have put Him to death if He had not desired to put Himself in the place of death.

The important fact about the death of Jesus Christ is that God the Father put Him to death. Nothing else is relevant; nothing else matters. All else is purely incidental; and while the incidental may be important, the great fact is that God the Father put God the Son to death. We read in the prophecy of Isaiah, "It pleased the Lord to bruise him; *he* hath put him to grief" (Isa. 53:10). And on the day of Pentecost Peter announced, "Ye men of Israel, hear these words, Jesus of Nazareth, a man approved of God among you by miracles and wonders and signs, which God did by him in the midst of you, as ye yourselves also know: Him, being delivered by the determinate counsel and foreknowledge of God, ye have taken, and by wicked hands have crucified and slain" (Acts 2:22,23). The important thing here is the declaration that Christ was delivered by the determinate counsel and foreknowledge of God. The evidence in the same chapter shows that the men who were thus accused, repented, received Christ as their Messiah and became the objects of God's saving grace. In all that happened at the cross there was forgiveness for men: all could be spared except Christ. God did not spare Him; God had to deliver Him up for us all (Rom. 8:32).

Chapter 4 of Romans is based on the theological implications of this fact. In this chapter Abraham is described as the man who believed the Word of God without wavering. He looked to the God who brings life out of death and calls things that are not as though they were. On this ground God reckoned Abraham's faith to him for righteousnes. God then announces that this righteousness is not only for Abraham but for us also, if we believe in God who raised up Jesus our Lord from the dead (vv. 23, 24). It must be noted that the emphasis is placed on the work of God the Father, acting as Judge. Note the striking difference in the expression used here concerning the death of Christ and that used in Romans 3, where the last ten verses show Jesus Christ as the propitiation — the mercy seat — through faith in His blood. The person and work of the Savior are revealed as the objects of our faith. The purpose of this mercy-seat sacrifice, we are told, is that God "might be just, and the justifier of him which believeth in Jesus" (Rom. 3:26). But in chapter 4 we look beyond Christ to God the Father who justified us through Christ.

To be truly justified, we must know not only the Savior who has paid the price, but the Father to whom the price has been paid. The order must be: first Christ, then the Father. The Lord Jesus said, "I am the way, the truth, and the life: no man cometh unto the Father, but by me" (John 14:6). Face to face with the God who justifies us, we are called to put our trust in Him who has completely dealt with our sins. To be truly justified we must know Him who has justified us.

We must see the Savior on the cross, then the Lord Jesus Christ risen and moving among His people. We must see Him seated on the throne of God, clothed in the glory He had with the Father before the world was. And when we see Him there, He will point us to the Father, who planned our redemption and accomplished it in every detail.

Our text (Rom. 4:25) does not say that Christ gave Himself for our sins but that He was delivered up because of our sins. It does not say that He rose because of our justification but that He was raised. In other passages in the Bible the Lord Jesus is the active performer; here He is presented as the passive victim. There is a double cause and a double effect.

First, we read that He was delivered because of our sins. The verb is a strong one, and has been translated by one commentator, "He was handed over because of our transgressions." In judicial procedure, a criminal who has been found guilty of murder is handed over to the hangman for execution. This is the idea in our text; it is the central idea in the epistle to the Romans. Jesus Christ was executed by God. This truth destroys all the false ideas that men have set forth in connection with the death of our Lord. This passage dissipates forever the governmental and exemplary theories of the atonement. Christ Jesus did not die as an example but as a substitute. He died in place of the believers.

A literal illustration of the substitutionary death of Christ, found in all four of the Gospels, shows this truth in a simple yet profound manner. In the accounts of the trial of Jesus, there is mention of one Barabbas, a notorious prisoner. In one Gospel he is described as a robber; another records that he was mixed up in an act of sedition in the city and that he had committed murder. On the occasion of the high Jewish festival, it was the custom to free one prisoner; so Pilate thought to get out of his predicament by releasing Jesus Christ, since the evidence showed no fault in Him. But the crowd insisted that Barabbas should be released and Jesus Christ should be crucified (Matt. 27:15-26; Mark 15:6-15; Luke 23:13-25; John 18:38-40). No less than thirty-eight verses in the four Gospels tell that simple story. It is significant that to the accounts of Barabbas half a dozen more verses are given than to all the accounts of the betrayal by Judas. Let us look at this man Barabbas.

In the first place, his name is pure Hebrew. *Bar* means son, and *abba* means father. Barabbas, then, means son of the father. Thus he represents all the sons of all the fathers who have ever begotten children. We are all of Adam's race, bound over for sedition against God. We rob Him of His glory. We are murderers of our souls and the souls of others. We find ourselves bound in the dark prison of sin. We merit the sentence that hangs over us and we wait, trembling, for the time of judgment. Every man loves freedom. To be put into a cell is a horrible curtailment of human liberty.

The Roman soldiers had stopped the riot and arrested Barabbas. His blood-guiltiness was established. He was flung into a cell to await execution. I have read several stories of the thoughts of prisoners before death. A man who is to be hanged has difficulty in keeping his hand away from his throat where the rope is so soon to choke him. In a prison where men are executed in a gas chamber, the condemned practice long breathing, and sometimes hold their breath until their eyes almost pop out. They know that they will hear the hissing sound of incoming death and that the breath they are now forcing into their lungs will be the last that they shall ever know. They hold on and on, straining at the thongs that tie them to their chair, until they are forced by the inexorable law of breathing to exhale their last breath and inhale the death that floats around them.

Barabbas must have looked at the palms of his hands and wondered how it would feel to have nails ripping through the flesh. He must have recalled seeing crucifixions, the slow agony of victims who suffered for a day or two before death released them. If he heard any hammering in the jail, he must have anticipated the sound of the clanging hammers that would bring death near to him. Then suddenly he hears the crowd outside, roaring. He thinks he hears his own name. He hears shouts; fear rises in his heart. Then he hears a key in the lock and the jailer releases him from the chain that binds him. He must have thought that his time had come, but the jailer takes him to the door and tells him that he is free.

In stupefaction he moves toward the crowd. There is scant welcome for him: he senses the deep preoccupation of the people. If he meets one of his old companions in the crowd, he is greeted with but a word. What overwhelms him is the surging roar, "Crucify Him! Crucify Him!" In modern language he would say to his companion, "What's the pitch? Give me the low-down." And he would be told that he has been released because Jesus is to be crucified instead of him.

Stunned, he walks nearer to the center of the scene and sees the Man who is to die in his place. Finally the procession begins toward Golgotha. He follows and sees Jesus fall under the weight of the cross. He sees Simon of Cyrene forced to carry the cross. Finally they arrive at Calvary. What must have been his thoughts? He hears the echoing blows of the hammer striking the nails, and he looks down at his own hands. This was to have been his day. Those nails were to have torn his flesh. But here he is, breathing the air of springtime and looking at the dark cloud gathering in the sky. We do not know whether or not he said, "Those hammer blows were meant for me, but He is dying in my place"; nevertheless it was for him literal substitution.

The cross is lifted up, and he sees the silhouette against the sky. The sun grows dark and he hears Christ say, "Father, forgive them, for they know not what they do." The centurion passes near him, and seeing the look upon the Savior's face says, "Truly this was the Son of God!" And Barabbas looks with wonder and amazement at the Man who is dying for him. There comes the cry, "It is finished!" and a little later he sees the body being taken down and put into its temporary grave. He goes back to the city, and all the little things that he had expected to see no more come before his eyes with the freshness of new creation. "He took my place! Jesus took my place! They released me, Barabbas, who deserved to die, and they crucified Jesus instead of me! He died instead of me!"

Now Barabbas was the only man in the world who could say that Jesus Christ took his physical place: but I can say that Jesus Christ

took my spiritual place. For I deserved to die. I deserved the wrath
of God, the eternal punishment of the lake of fire. Christ was
delivered up for my offenses, handed over to judgment because of
my sins. This is why we speak of the substitutionary atonement.
Christ was my substitute — He satisfied the debt of divine justice and
holiness. Christianity can be expressed in three phrases: I deserved
hell; Jesus took my hell; there is nothing left for me but His heaven.

Because He purchased heaven for me when He suffered on the
cross, God raised Him from the dead as a sign that the account was
settled in full. Note well that it was not that His resurrection produced our justification, but our justification produced His resurrection.
Our merited condemnation caused His death, and our accomplished
justification caused His resurrection.

The Swiss commentator, Frederick L. Godet, has a beautiful para-
graph on this point. He writes, "Our sin had killed Him; our
justification raised Him again. How so? The expiation of our
trespasses once accomplished by His death, and the right of God's
justice proved in earnest, God could pronounce the collective
acquittal of future believers, and He did so. . . . So long as the
security is in prison, the debt is not paid; the immediate *effect* of
payment would be his liberation. Similarly, if Jesus were not
raised, we should be more than ignorant whether our debt were paid;
we might be certain that it was not. His resurrection is the *proof*
of our justification, only because it is the necessary *effect* of it."

Every one of us at some time or other has walked into some office
to pay a bill for telephone service, for electricity, or some other obligation. We handed the money to the clerk who was appointed to act
for the company to which we were indebted. The clerk counted
the money, stamped the bill and handed us the receipt. The company
could never collect that bill again for we could produce the receipt
to prove that the debt was paid and that we were free from the obligation forever. The Lord Jesus Christ walked up to Calvary, God's
desk for the payment of the bill for our sins. The account was heavy
against us, and the Lord Jesus Christ could settle it only by dying
for us. There was no other means of settlement. He offered His
life; and God the Father took that life, handed it over to His justice
for execution, and His holiness turned away from the scene, leaving

the Savior alone to cry out, "My God, my God, why hast thou forsaken me?" (Matt. 27:46). When three hours of daylight and three hours of darkness were ended, payment had been made in full. So far as God was concerned, those hours were eternal. He does not reckon time as we count it; for Him one day is as a thousand years and a thousand years as but a day. For God the Father and God the Son, those three hours of light and three hours of darkness comprised all the days and nights of all the years of time and eternity. Christ suffered eternal punishment for everyone chosen in Christ before the foundation of the world.

After Christ died, His friends took His body and reverently cared for it, putting it into the tomb, wrapping it in linen with myrrh, the symbol of death. But it was not possible for the Lord Jesus Christ to be held by death. He had paid the complete debt, and the Lord God Almighty reached out, as a cashier might stamp a bill, "Paid in Full," and raised His Son from the dead, for there was nothing more to pay.

"Jesus paid it all," we sing, and it is the truth about the cross. The resurrection is the receipt for the bill.

While a guest in the house of Gaius, a Roman Christian living in Corinth, Paul dictated his letter to the Romans, saying that Christ was delivered up and that He was raised up. When did this occur? About twenty-five years before Paul wrote. Where? On Calvary's hill outside of Jerusalem. Bishop Handley Moule says, "There were at that moment about three hundred known living people, at least (1 Cor. 15:6), who had seen the Risen One with open eyes, and heard Him with conscious ears. From one point of view, all was eternal, spiritual, invisible. From another point of view our salvation was as concrete, as historical, as much a thing of place and date, as the battle of Actium, or the death of Socrates. And what was done, remains done." *historical fact - Ress.*

He was delivered up because of my offenses, my sins, my transgressions. And because God justified me and counted the bill as paid in full, forever, the Lord Jesus Christ was raised from the dead.

Chapter Nine

THE EXALTED CHRIST

We have seen how God the Father put God the Son, the Lord Jesus Christ, to death. We must keep in mind that this was not an enforced death. You and I have to die because of sin. The Lord Jesus Christ died because He loved to do the Father's will. The wages of sin was death and God had the Lord Jesus Christ die in our stead that we might have everlasting life. He did not die as a martyr for a lost cause; willingly He came to earth to die. Thus we read in the Word of God concerning Him: "Consequently, when Christ came into the world, he said, Sacrifices and offerings thou hast not desired, but a body hast thou prepared for me; in burnt offerings and sin offerings thou hast taken no pleasure. Then I said, 'Lo, I have come to do thy will, O God,' as it is written of me in the roll of the book" (Heb. 10:5-7).

But the Lord Jesus Christ knew that the cross was not the end of the road. He knew that after the cross there would be the crown. He knew that though the Father would put Him to death, the Father would cause Him to rise again. All through His life the crown was ever before Him. This was His joy — to do the Father's will even though it meant the cross. He said: "For this reason the Father loves me, because I lay down my life, that I may take it again. No one takes it from me, but I lay it down of my own accord. I have power to lay it down, and I have power to take it again; this charge I have received from my Father" (John 10:17,18). And we might well note that He emphasizes the fact that this power over life and death was given to Him by the Father.

Coming to the close of His ministry, on that night when He prayed alone in the garden, the Lord Jesus petitioned the Father: "I glorified thee on earth, having accomplished the work which thou gavest me to do; and now, Father, glorify thou me in thy own presence with the glory which I had with thee before the world was made" (John 17:4,5). And as the Son was faithful to the Father even unto death, the Father was faithful even to raising Him from the dead. Thus exalted by God the Father, He is given a new position, He is given a new name, and He is made pre-eminent above all things.

Paul, in endeavoring to describe the power of God to the Ephesian believers, does so in terms of the resurrection of Christ. He writes: "The eyes of your understanding being enlightened; that ye may know what is the hope of his calling, and what the riches of the glory of his inheritance in the saints, And what is the exceeding greatness of his power to us-ward who believe, according to the working of his mighty power, Which he wrought in Christ, when he raised him from the dead, and set him at his own right hand in the heavenly places, Far above all principalities, and power, and might, and dominion, and every name that is named, not only in this world, but also in that which is to come" (Eph. 1:18-21).

Here we see the mighty strength of the power of God. It is a power which can conquer death; it is a power which can raise Christ to God's own right hand; it is a power which makes Him superior over every might and dominion in this world and in the world to come. It is that power which alone is sufficient to take the divine Son back from an earthly grave to a heavenly throne.

And because of this, all things have been put under His feet. No more can things defeat Him. No more can anyone humiliate

Him. He is the supreme head — the Head of the Church, which is His body, the fullness of Him that fills all in all.

And accompanying this exalted position as Head of the Church, He, the risen Lord Jesus, is given a new name. It is a victorious name for at its sound every knee will bow. We read in the epistle to the Philippians: "Wherefore God also hath highly exalted him, and given him a name which is above every name: that at the name of Jesus every knee should bow, of things in heaven, and things in earth, and things under the earth; And that every tongue should confess that Jesus Christ is Lord, to the glory of God the Father" (Phil. 2:9-11). There is influence in a name. There are influential names in finance, science, theology — in all fields of human endeavor. But the greatest name, the most influential name, the name of victory and power is that of our risen Lord Jesus Christ before whom every knee shall bow. It is a name which befits His exalted position, since He is far above principalities and powers. It is fitting that these principalities and powers — these things in heaven and in earth, these things in the present world and the world to come — should bow at the naming of this name. Today He is despised and rejected; He is blasphemed; He is set aside. But the day will come when every tongue shall confess that Jesus Christ is Lord to the glory of God the Father.

Men may say that Jesus died on the cross as a martyr for a lost cause. But the day will come when they will change their opinion, for they shall see that on the cross He died to do the Father's will.

The Lord Jesus Christ was rejected because of man's rebellion. God the Father desired that God the Son should be made pre-eminent. The purpose of the exaltation of the Son is to deliver Him from the humiliation that man passed upon Him. This is why Paul writes to the Colossians: "He is before all things, and in him all things hold together. He is the head of the body, the church; he is the beginning, the firstborn from the dead, that in everything he might be pre-eminent. For in him all the fulness of God was pleased to dwell" (Col. 1:17-19). In these verses the Apostle Paul gives us the scope of this exaltation. First, as the agent of creation He was before all things, and the purpose of all things is to glorify Him, for it is He who sustains all things now. But not only as creator is He pre-eminent.

He is pre-eminent as redeemer, the redeemer who not only died but who rose from the dead. This is the glory of His pre-eminence. This is the marvel of His exaltation.

But lest someone think that the truth of His exaltation is but an abstract doctrine, let us now consider the practical effects of His exaltation, first for the believer and then for those who have never trusted in the Lord Jesus Christ as their own personal Savior.

Through the exaltation of the Lord Jesus Christ as manifested by His resurrection we have been reconciled to God. We must never forget that our sins estranged us from, cut us off from, and made us dead toward, God. But yet in marvelous love God found a way to redeem us and bring us back to Himself. Continuing in his letter to the Colossians Paul writes: "And through him to reconcile to himself all things, whether on earth or in heaven, making peace by the blood of his cross. And you, who once were estranged and hostile in mind, doing evil deeds, he has now reconciled in his body of flesh by his death, in order to present you holy and blameless and irreproachable before him" (Col. 1:20-22). His exaltation is an eternal guarantee that sin need not separate us from God any longer. Let us remember, however, that the separation was deep and wide. Paul describes its nature when writing to the Ephesians: "You were ... separated from Christ, alienated from the commonwealth of Israel, and strangers to the covenants of promise, having no hope and without God in the world. But now in Christ Jesus you who once were far off have been brought near in the blood of Christ" (Eph. 2:12,13).

We can never appreciate the practical results of Christ's exaltation if we do not know the vastness of our separation from God. Many times during my ministry people have come to my study in my church in Philadelphia to ask me to pray for them. Often I had the suspicion that they were not born again. They would come and say, "Dr. Barnhouse, will you pray for my son who is in the armed forces on the battlefields in Europe?" I would reply, "How can I pray for you or for your son?" They would quickly ask, "Are you not a minister? Isn't it your business to pray? We come to your church." And then I would say to them, "But you see, God hasn't promised you one thing. God hasn't promised to take care of your son. There is only one way for you to pray to Him — through the Lord Jesus Christ." Their faces would drop and they would become very, very serious. They loved their son. They desired his protection. But I made it definitely clear to them that there was only one way to the heart of God and that was through the heart of the Lord Jesus Christ. We must never forget that He Himself said, "I am the way, the truth, and the life: no man cometh unto the Father, but by me" (John 14:6). However, I was always happy to tell such people that in the exaltation of the Lord Jesus Christ I could bring them the good news that Christ died for them and that He would provide them an access to God the Father if they would come to Him trusting Him as their living Savior and Lord.

Not only has He reconciled us to God but His exaltation bears testimony to the fact that He is at the right hand of God interceding for us as our advocate. How many times do we need someone at the throne of grace to plead our case! We are overwhelmed by the world, we are confused by our own ignorance, we do stupid things due to our rebellious wills, and yet even before we call there is an advocate at God's right hand making intercession for us. This is the blessing of His exaltation.

John writes: "My little children, I am writing this to you so that you may not sin; but if anyone does sin, we have an advocate with the Father, Jesus Christ the righteous; and He is the expiation [propitiation] for our sins, and not for ours only, but also for the sins of the whole world" (1 John 2:1,2). This is why we never need to appear before the throne of grace in great fright or terror. This is why we never need to come as strangers to an unknown god, as criminals before a judge. This is why we can come as children to our heavenly Father through our advocate, the righteous, risen Lord Jesus Christ.

The exaltation of the Lord Jesus Christ has redeemed me and taken care of my past, has given me an advocate with whom I may live in the present, and has provided me with a living hope which assures me of a fearless future. Peter writes of this glorious hope in his first epistle. "Blessed be the God and Father of our Lord Jesus Christ! By his great mercy we have been born anew to a living hope through the resurrection of Jesus Christ from the dead, and to an inheritance which is imperishable, undefiled, and unfading, kept in heaven for you, who by God's power are guarded through faith for a salvation ready to be revealed in the last time" (1 Pet. 1:3-5).

Because God by His marvelous power raised Jesus Christ from the dead, we have the promise that we, too, shall be raised from the dead since we possess the glorious hope of which the Apostle Peter speaks. Well might we examine the words by which he describes it in verse 4. It is *imperishable*. It is *undefiled*. It is *unfading*. This hope is steadfast, for it is anchored in the Lord Jesus Christ. It will never prove to be a mirage. We shall never be disillusioned by it. And verse 5 brings to our mind the truth that not only is this hope indestructible but we are preserved for it.

Some time ago I learned of a Christian family which was struck by tragedy. One of the sons, a brilliant boy, having finished his studies and about to enter his career, was killed in an accident. The father, a minister, from his meager income had saved for the boy's education. The boy had been sickly and so there had also been medical expenses. Through it all the father had looked forward to the time when his son would enter the ministry. Nothing was too much to prepare for this day. And just as the day was about to dawn the boy was taken Home to be with the Lord. There the father had a glorious hope but he had no son to realize it. It is a wonderful thing for us to know that not only have we been born again to a living hope which can never, never pass away but we are preserved for that hope until the day when we shall see our Lord face to face. Because of this blessed hope I heard that father say as he stood beside the casket of his son that the sufferings of this present world were not worthy to be compared with the glory that should follow. This is what the exaltation of our Lord Jesus Christ means to the believer. We stand in Christ knowing that He is our present advocate even as we await the time, the hour, when we shall see Him as He is.

But what does the exaltation of our Lord Jesus Christ mean to those who do not know Him? First of all, the exaltation of Christ makes it possible for us to say that they may know the good news of salvation. The great Christmas message announced this news. When He was born a babe in Bethlehem, the angels said, "Behold, I bring you good tidings of great joy, which shall be to all people. For unto you is born this day in the city of David a Savior, which is Christ the Lord" (Luke 2:10,11). And whosoever shall call upon the name of the Lord shall be saved. Because of the exaltation of Christ, God wrote through John: "For God so loved the world, that he gave his only begotten Son, that whosoever believeth in him should not perish, but have everlasting life" (John 3:16). However, if men refuse the pardoning grace of God the Father, the exaltation of the Lord Jesus Christ will spell only tragedy for them. When Christ came the first time in humiliation, He came to be the Savior of the world. But when He comes apart from sin the second time unto salvation, He will come as the world's Judge. In the Gospel of John we read: "For as the Father has life in himself, so he has granted the Son also to have life in himself, and has given him authority to execute judgment, because he is the Son of man. Do not marvel at this; for the hour is coming when all who are in the tombs shall hear his voice and come forth, those who have done good, to the resurrection of life, and those who have done evil, to the resurrection of judgment" (John 5:26-29). Our Lord Jesus Christ is given this office of judge because of the exaltation which has been bestowed upon Him by God the Father. In this same passage our Lord said that He could do nothing on His own authority but as He hears so He judges. His judgment is just, because He did not seek His own will but the will of the Father.

Today the people of the world seem to have great pleasure in rejecting Christ. They take pleasure in evil, ignoring the fact that a day of judgment will come. Because of the seeming silence of God, which they interpret as indifference to their evil, they go on their way unaware of the doom which is impending. Paul refers to this when writing to the Romans. He calls to their minds that God's silence is not to be interpreted as indifference; it is a sign of His goodness intending to lead men to repentance. But there will come a day when the secrets of every man's heart will be revealed. No longer will men use one another for their evil deeds nor will they be able to make excuses. Everyone will be silent and will know beyond the question of doubt that he is guilty before God.

And when will this great judgment take place? It is described in the closing chapters of the Book of the Revelation: "Then I saw a great white throne and him who sat upon it; from his presence earth and sky fled away, and no place was found for them. And I saw the dead, great and small, standing before the throne, and books were opened. Also another book was opened, which is the book of life. And the dead were judged by what was written in the books, by what they had done. And the sea gave up the dead in it, Death and Hades gave up the dead in them, and all were judged by what they had done. Then Death and Hades were thrown into the lake of fire. This is the second death . . . and if anyone's name was not found written in the book of life, he was thrown into the lake of fire" (Rev. 20:11-15).

A careful study of this text shows that the judgment is not arbitrary. In fact, even in the midst of this last judgment, God endeavors to show mercy and grace. All who have rejected the Lord Jesus Christ are brought before God's judgment seat. Three books are opened; the Register of the Damned, the Book of Their Works, and the Book of Life. As their names are called from the first volume, they stand before their Judge who might well have been their Savior. They are permitted to plead their case as the Savior-Judge listens to their plea. In their defense they turn to the second volume whereby their life works are reviewed. It is in condescending grace that the Lord Jesus Christ seeks to find something to commend them to Him. But there is nothing. Paul is confirmed where he states in Romans, "There is none righteous, no, not one. . . . There is none that seeketh after God. They are become unprofitable. . . . For all have sinned, and come short of the glory of God" (Rom. 3:10-12,23). This tragic statement closes the great tribunal: "And if any one's name was not found written in the book of life, he was thrown into the lake of fire." The tragedy is, that on this great day of final judgment, those who reject the Lord Jesus Christ now will not be found written in the Book of Life then.

And to those of you who may not know our Lord Jesus Christ, we would not have you think that we rejoice in this final judgment. We do not! Our great desire is that you shall come to know the risen Lord who has been exalted by the Father. And in this spirit of the Apostle Paul we appeal to you now: "God was in Christ reconciling the world to himself, not counting their trespasses against them, and entrusting to us the message of reconciliation. So we are ambassadors for Christ, God making his appeal through us. We beseech you on behalf of Christ, be reconciled to God" (2 Cor. 5:19, 20). Our desire is that the exaltation of our Lord Jesus Christ prove a triumph for you, not a tragedy. Why not accept Him now?

PART THREE

THE GRACE OF THE LIVING CHRIST
"Be Reconciled to God"

Are you still dead in trespasses and sin? Have you never experienced new life in Christ? If you have once known Christ, do you know how to be restored to fellowship with Him? Look to the promises of God; and look at His gift, the Crucified Risen Lord.

Chapter Ten

THE PROMISES OF GOD

Suppose you are given a large block of very valuable stock. You want to turn the stock into money but you have no knowledge of finance. And so you stare helplessly at the stock certificates and wish you had the money. Now many Christians are like that when they read God's promises in the Bible. They read a promise and they say, "How wonderful!" But they do not know how to cash in on the promise and to benefit by it in daily life.

There is no situation in the life of any believer that has not been provided for by promises in the Word of God. To prove this, here are four promises that cover every situation in life. First, Romans 8:32 says, "He who did not spare his own Son but gave him up for us all, will he not also give us all things with him?" Ephesians 1:3 tells us that God "has blessed us in Christ with every spiritual blessing in the heavenly places." Third, in Matthew 6:33 Christ says, "Seek first his [God's] kingdom and his righteousness, and all these things shall be yours as well." And fourth, in Psalm 84:11 God says, "No good thing does the Lord withhold from those who walk uprightly." These four promises cover all that the human

87

heart could desire. But how are we to capitalize on these promises? How shall we cash them?

First, you must recognize what your need is and then search the Word of God for the promise that meets your need. As a boy in my teens I had the privilege of studying under Dr. Reuben A. Torrey. One day he was teaching on James 1:5, which says: "If any of you lacks wisdom, let him ask God who gives to all men generously and without reproaching." Dr. Torrey asked the students, "What must you first do in order to get wisdom?" Many replied, "Ask"; and no one guessed the right answer. Finally, Dr. Torrey pointed out that the promise begins with the words, "If any of you lacks wisdom, let him ask God." So in order for God to give you wisdom you must first realize that you have no wisdom.

Many people do not have the wisdom of God simply because they do not think that they need it. They think that they can get along all right as they are. Now analyze your life in the office, the store, the shop, the factory or in social relationships. Do you not just sort of muddle through? "Well," you say, "I use common sense!" But the Bible flatly says that you are never to use your common sense. In Proverbs 3:5 we read, "Trust in the Lord with all your heart, and do not rely on your own insight"; lean not on your own understanding, your own common sense. The Christian must become familiar with the promises. Just as a child must become familiar with various coins, so the Christian must know the promises of God for various situations.

Have you ever wondered why some people enter church and come out better, while others come out worse? The answer is found in two verses joined together: Hebrews 4:2 and 1 Thessalonians 2:13. The first says, "For good news came to us just as to them; but the message which they heard did not benefit them, because it did not meet with faith in the hearers." The second says, "When you received the word of God which you heard from us, you accepted it not as the word of men but as what it really is, the word of God, which is at work in you believers."

In other words, it is as though everyone carried a bowl to church, and the preacher pours his sermon into each bowl. In some cases it is retained, and in others it splashes out. The Bible says that if you carry faith in your bowl, the message will benefit you. If you pray, "Lord, I want to be fed, I want to grow, I want to understand Your Word and live by it," then God's Word will be a blessing to you, and you will leave the service a better Christian. But if you do not open your heart and submit yourself to God's Word, He cannot bless you. It is written of the Lord Jesus that He did not do many mighty works in a certain town because of their unbelief (Matt. 13:58).

I want to divide God's promises into several groups and show you how they apply to different needs in life. First, young believers must know the promises of salvation because they give assurance. When I was about fifteen, I experienced assurance of salvation. And then when I slipped and stumbled in some way, the devil said to me, "You've had an evil thought! You just lost your temper! Are you *really* saved?" I wondered whether the awareness of sin proved that I really was not saved. I got down on my knees and said, "Lord, if I didn't do it right the first time, I'll do it all over and I'll accept Christ as my Savior right now!"

Of course I was saved; but what I needed and what every new Christian needs is the knowledge of God's promises and how to apply them. That is the way to answer Satan. We need such a promise as Romans 8:1: "There is therefore now no condemnation for those who are in Christ Jesus." Oh, what a promise this is! And again in Acts 13:39, "By him [Christ] every one that believes is freed from everything from which you could not be freed by the law of Moses." Ephesians 2:8,9: "For by grace you have been saved through faith; and this is not your own doing, it is the gift of God — not because of works, lest any man should boast!" Titus 3:5: "He saved us, not because of deeds done by us in righteousness, but in virtue of his own mercy, by the washing of regeneration and renewal in the Holy Spirit." We all know John 3:16, "For God so loved the world that he gave his only Son, that whoever believes in him should not perish but have eternal life."

And then there is the promise that I think is the greatest of all in the Bible: Romans 4:5: "To one who does not work but trusts him who justifies the ungodly, his faith is reckoned as righteousness." In other words, God takes a man who is dead in trespasses and sin, makes him alive, and says, "I count him as righteous." Oh, how wonderful to have such promises when sin first comes to us after we have believed! We can say, "There is the promise in the Word of God. I'm saved, the Word of God says so, for it is here that I met the Lord Jesus Christ!"

In the second place, we need to know the promises that God will pardon us when we sin and will maintain us in fellowship with Himself. You see, an unsaved man has only the nature of Adam; but the Christian has two natures, the nature of Adam, and the nature of Christ Himself. We have been made partakers of the divine nature, but even though we are saved, the Adamic nature is still present to drag us down. Day by day we must deal with the sin which arises from the old nature. How wonderful, therefore, is such a promise as 1 John 1:9: "If we confess our sins, he is faithful and just, and will forgive our sins and cleanse us from all unrighteousness." Now when you are aware that you have sinned, you may turn at once to God and say, "O Father, I have sinned and I need cleansing." And at once He will cleanse you and restore you to fellowship with Himself.

In the third place, we need the promises that tell us that God will never forsake His people, that we are His through all eternity, and that it is impossible to fall away and be lost. Philippians 1:6 is such a promise: "Being confident of this very thing, that he who has begun a good work in you will bring it to perfection in the day of Jesus Christ." In Hebrews 13:5 God says, "I will never fail you nor forsake you." In the original Greek this verse has three negatives to express how impossible it is for God to forsake us. It is perhaps the strongest set of negatives in one sentence in all Scripture — "Never, never, never forsake you." The poet who wrote the great hymn, "How Firm a Foundation," must have read this passage.

Then we need such a promise as John 10:27-29: "My sheep hear my voice, and I know them, and they follow me; and I give them" . . . six months' life? That would be no gospel at all! Rather, it is, "My sheep hear my voice, and I know them, and they follow me; and I give them *eternal life,* and they shall never perish, and no one shall snatch them out of my hand. My Father, who has given them to me, is greater than all, and no one is able to snatch them out of the Father's hand."

In one of my early books I tell the story of a little boy who was asked, "But aren't you afraid you'll slip through His fingers?" And the child replied, "I am one of the fingers." How wonderful, that when we are born again we become members of the Body of Christ. No one can amputate us from Him.

Someone may ask, "Do you mean that so long as you believe in Christ you can live as you please?" Of course not! Far from it! Because you *are* in the Body of Christ, you are to behave as a member of His Body should. A man who owned a flock of prize sheep explained to me how each lamb's ear is notched at birth in a special way in order to identify that lamb. I said, "So your sheep are marked in the ear. Did you know that the Lord's sheep are marked in both the ear and the foot?" He asked, "What do you mean?" I said, "Here it says, 'My sheep *hear* my voice. . . and they *follow* me.' The moment we are saved, we receive the ability to hear Christ's voice as we read the Bible, and to walk in the way that He wants us to go."

Not only do we need the promises of salvation, pardon, and assurance of God's faithfulness, but we need a fourth set of promises which assure us of daily victory over sin. Oh, what a wonderful promise is Romans 6:14! "Sin will have no dominion over you, since you are not under law but under grace." And again, Galatians 5:17, 18: "The desires of the flesh are against the Spirit, and the desires of the Spirit are against the flesh; for these are opposed to each other. . . . But if you are led by the Spirit you are not under the law." And what a tremendous promise is 1 Corinthians 10:13: "No temptation has overtaken you that is not common to man. God is faithful, and he will not let you be tempted beyond your strength, but with the temptation will also provide the way of escape, that you may be able to endure it." You see, these are guarantees that Satan will not get you all the way down and triumph over you (cf. Ps. 37:23, 24).

In a wrestling match the rules are that the winner must pin down three of four points — two hips and two shoulder blades. Three of these four must be against the mat. God promises that although Satan may get you two points down once in a while, the Christian will never be put three points down. You may be buffeted, you may be thrown, but then is the time to say, "Lord, Lord! See where sin has brought me!" And just there the Lord Jesus rescues you, cleanses you, and makes you strong. These are the great promises of victory.

I once heard the story of the dear old colored man who lived such a life of triumph with the Lord that he was asked, "What do you do when you are tempted?" He answered, "I just pray, 'Lord, your property is in danger!'" And we are His property. He has redeemed us at such a price that He will take care of us; He loves us, and will bring us through. We shall never be gotten three points down.

In another set of promises, God tells us that He gives grace to live a life that is pleasing to Him. He says, "I will instruct you and teach you the way you should go; I will guide you with mine eye" (Ps. 32:8). He will definitely guide us. In Isaiah 30:21 He says, "Your ears shall hear a word behind you, saying, 'This is the way, walk in it,' when you turn to the right or when you turn to the left." And there is the promise that He will cleanse and keep our whole being for Himself. Paul wrote to the Thessalonians, "May the God of peace himself sanctify you wholly; and may your spirit and soul and body be kept sound and blameless at the coming of our Lord Jesus Christ. He who calls you is faithful, and he will do it" (1 Thess. 5:23,24).

God also promises that He will comfort us in every trial and difficulty. John 14:16 tells us that He will send us another Comforter who will guide us into all truth. What a wonderful promise that is. And by "Comforter" He does not mean a downy quilt, for the word "comforter" comes from Latin: *con*, "with," and *fortis*, "strong." A "comforter" is one who comes with strength. This is the original meaning: *with strength*. So the Holy Spirit, our Comforter, strengthens us to face life.

In this matter of comfort, 2 Corinthians 1:3,4 is the most comforting passage in all the Bible. For there we read: "Blessed be the God and Father of our Lord Jesus Christ, the Father of mercies and the God of all comfort" — isn't that a wonderful name for God, "the God of all comfort"? — "who comforts us in all our affliction, so that we may be able to comfort those who are in any affliction, with the comfort with which we ourselves are comforted by God." Isn't that a lot of comfort? When a loved one dies, God says, "You do not grieve as others do who have no hope. You do not sorrow as others who have no hope" (1 Thess. 4:13). And to those who suffer physical agony, how wonderful is 2 Corinthians 12:9: "My grace is sufficient for you, for my strength is made perfect in weakness."

Then there are the promises that God will supply all our needs. Philippians 4:19 says, "My God will supply every need of yours according to his riches in glory in Christ Jesus." He does not promise to supply all your *greed*, but all your *need*. Have you ever heard a mother say, "That child needs a spanking"? Well, God will provide spankings, as well as breakfast, dinner, and supper. You have heard a father say, "Oh, I'm going to take care of that boy!" And God will take care of you with spankings as well as with more pleasant favors. King Solomon wrote, "My son, do not despise the Lord's discipline or be weary of his reproof, for the Lord reproves him whom he loves, as a father the son in whom he delights" (Prov. 3:11,12).

So here in God's Word are His promises which we can appropriate right now — promises of salvation, of pardon, of God's faithfulness, of victory over sin, of power, of comfort, of provision for every need. These are the assets which God has given to us.

The most wonderful phase of the promises of God is that they are all for each believer. When I was a young pastor in southern France during my university days, there was a lovely French girl of a fine family who came to our house almost every day and spent as much time as she could with my wife. She was learning English and the answers to problems in the Christian life. We had a promise box which greatly intrigued her. Two or three hundred Bible verses had been printed, each on a small piece of heavy paper; then they had been rolled tightly into a cylinder about the thickness of a pencil and an inch long. These were placed together in a small box and at table each person drew a promise and read it aloud. Simone was so delighted with this that she made one by hand with the promises copied in French from her Bible.

Many years passed. The Second World War came and went. We visited her and her husband, a pastor in southern France. She told of all the deprivations of the war, the German occupation and finally the terrors of the liberation. The Germans had forced special paper money on the country, and in the terrible days after the Americans landed in the south the Germans began to retreat rapidly, destroying many things as they left. The German occupation money wasn't worth the paper it was printed on. The farmers stayed in the country and did not bring food into the town markets. She had a family of small children and they were practically starving. There was no money except the German money which no one would accept. A restaurant keeper gave her a peck of potato peelings each day and she boiled them for her family. The children were hungry and crying. The mother, pale and emaciated, had come to the breaking point.

Weeping, she went into her bedroom and picked up the old box of promises which she had cherished through the years. She cried out, "O Lord, I am at the absolute end. You *must* give me a promise for this moment." She turned towards her bed with the thought of kneeling beside it to pray. The box tipped and all of the promises scattered on the bed and on the floor where she had fallen to her knees. A rush of joy and triumph came over her as she realized that she was to have, not one promise which would be pulled from the box, but all the promises, plus all those which were not in the box.

Learn this great lesson. All the promises, yes, all the promises are for us Yea and Amen in Christ (2 Cor. 1:20). There is no word in all the Bible that cannot be understood as belonging to you this instant. Ask the Holy Spirit to apply the Word to your heart.

Chapter Eleven

FALLING INTO GRACE

When we understand the nature of our salvation, we understand why we cannot lose it. Salvation does not instantly change a man; rather it is the planting of a new life alongside the old. We are justified, made righteous, in Christ. Justification is a new creation. Sanctification is the lifelong process of Christian growth. When the day of glorification comes, we shall have new bodies; the old nature of sin will be gone, and we shall be with Christ and be like Him forever. We need to understand, however, that salvation is not accomplished by adding to what a man already has until he meets God's standard; it is entirely the work of God. We must avoid the heresy of thinking that if a man is 10 per cent good, he needs only 90 per cent from God; and if he is 50 per cent good, he needs 50 per cent to be supplied by God; if he is 70 per cent good, he needs only 30 per cent from God. The good man must abandon his 70 per cent and receive 100 percent from God. The average man must turn his back on his 50 per cent and get 100 per cent from God. And the criminal must get a new 100 per cent from God.

Another error to avoid is to think that when we believe in Jesus our sins are forgiven from the time we are born up to that moment but that thereafter we must work it out for ourselves. God does not justify a man over a period of fifteen years, if the man is fifteen when he believes in Christ. When a person trusts in Christ, God justifies him in his entire personal history, so that when a man is saved he is saved from his past, his present and his future. He is looked upon as being in Christ:

> Dressed in His righteousness alone;
> Faultless to stand before the Throne.

God deals with the man in the totality of his experience and counts the man as being in Christ. He is therefore a new creation. Certain objections are brought against this doctrine because some people think it is possible to be lost again after being saved, and then to be saved and lost again. They hold the notion that one can "fall from grace." They say, "Oh, look at so and so! He was a Christian, but he fell from grace!"

Now the phrase "fallen from grace" occurs only once in the Bible, in the fifth chapter of Galatians. If we read it in its context, we shall see that one falls from grace not by what he does but by what he thinks, and that falling from grace has nothing to do with salvation. Galatians 5:1,2 says: "Stand fast therefore in the liberty wherewith Christ hath made us free, and be not entangled again with the yoke of bondage. Now I, Paul, say to you that if you receive circumcision, Christ will be of no advantage to you." Paul was writing to those who had been influenced by Jewish Christians, brought up in the form and ceremony of the old Jewish faith. They argued that faith in Christ alone was not sufficient for salvation. Circumcision here stands for any works or self-effort, such as baptism or keeping the Sabbath, as a supplement to what Jesus Christ did. We could paraphrase Paul's words, "If you receive baptism with the thought that baptism can save you, Christ will be of no advantage to you," because it is akin to saying that the death of the Son of God on the cross of Calvary 1900 years ago is not enough; I must perform some church ritual and thus earn my way into heaven. That is what is meant by falling from grace, for Galatians 5:3 says, "I testify again to every man who receives circumcision [or is baptized

for salvation, or keeps the Sabbath for salvation] that he is bound
to keep the whole law." Returning to my earlier illustration, if you
want to be saved by works you must produce 100 per cent. God
says, "I won't settle for 99 and 44/100." "But," you say, "I cannot produce 100 per cent goodness." "All right," says God, "abandon
everything and come to the cross, and I will give you My righteousness
for nothing. The moment you admit that you deserve hell but
that I loved you and sent My Son to die for you, I will admit you to
My family and you will be with Me in heaven forever. But if you
refuse to accept My terms and insist on trying to satisfy Me with
your own good works, I must keep you out of heaven. It is all, or
nothing at all."

Galatians 5:4 is the heart of our message: "You are severed from
Christ, you who would be justified by the law; you have fallen
away from grace." Now I have heard people pervert this verse to
mean that a Christian falls from grace when he commits sin. They
say, "Oh, he fell from grace!" He did not. Suppose a man who
used to get drunk three times a week is born again; after eight
months of abstinence he gets drunk again. Has he fallen from
grace? You do not fall from grace by sinning. It is wrong to get
drunk, of course. God has flatly stated, "Do not get drunk with
wine, for that is debauchery; but be filled with the Spirit" (Eph. 5:18).
God will undoubtedly deal with one who commits that sin against
his own body. But from the point of view of the Bible you do *not*
fall from grace by sinning. If you fall out of your window you fall
into your garden. If you fall out of grace you fall into law. You
fall from grace by turning back to salvation by law, contrary to grace,
and in favor of man's efforts. God does it all, or you do it alone.
God will *never* deal with a person who says, "Well, I'll do the best
I can, and God can do the rest." God wants none of our self-
effort. On the cross He gave Jesus Christ for our sins. There
Jesus paid the full price for our salvation. Now I am not saying
that you are not to live the Christian life after you are saved. But
you must comprehend that love so amazing, so divine, has given us
everything. What God asks is that, as Paul writes in 2 Corinthians
5:9, "We make it our aim to please him."

When you learn what you fall into when you fall from grace,

you will never think that you lose salvation by falling into sin. However, the last thing I want to do is to give comfort to someone who might say, "Well if that is so, I can live as I please." No, you cannot! For when one appreciates the grace of God, he will take care how he lives; he will want to please God who is the possessor of heaven and earth.

No! When a child of God sins, he does not fall from grace, but he falls *into* grace! Let me illustrate this truth by the following story. Sir Edward C. Burne-Jones was a prominent artist in England during the latter part of the nineteenth century. One day Sir Edward went to tea at the home of his daughter, and as a special treat his little grand-daughter was allowed to come to the table. But she became naughty, and her mother made her stand in the corner with her face to the wall. Now Sir Edward, being a well-trained grandfather, did not interfere with his grandchild's training. But next morning he arrived at his daughter's home with paints and palette. He went to the wall where the little girl had stood and there he painted pictures — a kitten chasing its tail; lambs in a field; goldfish swimming. The wall on both sides of that corner was decorated with his paintings, all for his grand-daughter's delight. If she had to stand in the corner again, at least she would have something to look at.

When a Christian commits sin and is put into a corner, God does not send him to hell. Instead God paints pictures to illustrate His love and grace. Let us talk to men of the past and see the pictures God painted for them.

Abraham, were you a child of God? "Oh, yes, praise God!" Did God justify you? "Yes, He did." Did you sin after you trusted God? "Oh, yes, I played the fool. I taught my wife Sarah to lie and to say she was my sister. I was willing to sacrifice her honor to save my skin." Well, Abraham, did you fall from grace? "Fall from grace? I fell *into* grace! God put me into a corner and painted pictures on my wall. He painted the fair land of Canaan and said, 'Go in and possess the land. I have given this land to you and to your seed after you for-ever.' He painted stars and sand and said, 'Your children shall be as the stars in the sky and the sand of the sea.'"

Jacob, did you sin after you became a believer? "Oh, yes! my very name Jacob means supplanter, crook. And was I crooked! I cheated my brother out of his blessing by impersonating him and giving my blind father a stew of goat's meat." Did you fall from grace? "Fall from grace? I had to run away to keep from being murdered, but how I fell *into* grace! God put me into a corner, but on the wall he painted pictures, a ladder from earth to heaven, with angels going up and down on it. I called that corner 'Bethel'—House of God, the gate of heaven."

Moses, you were a believer and God's appointed servant. Did you ever sin after you became a believer? "I was brought up in Pharaoh's palace and thought I was pretty important. When an Egyptian fought with a Hebrew, I murdered the Egyptian and fled from Egypt." Did you fall from grace? "Fall from grace? God put me into a corner and forty years later He painted a burning bush on my wall and said, 'Put off your shoes from your feet, for the place on which you are standing is holy ground.' And then He sent me back to Egypt to lead His people out of bondage and to give them His holy law."

David, take the witness stand. You were a believer and God's anointed king. Did you sin? "Yes, I did. When I should have been leading my army to battle, I stayed home and committed adultery with another man's wife. Then I had her husband murdered." David, did you fall from grace? "Fall from grace? Oh! God put me into a corner, and on the wall He painted green pastures and still waters, a shepherd and sheep; and He said, 'I have made a covenant with David my servant.' I fell *into* grace."

Now let us call a New Testament believer. Peter, did you sin after you followed the Lord Jesus Christ? "Oh," says Peter, "what a fool I was! I was just a little two-by-four fisherman from Galilee. I traveled with Jesus; He was so wonderful and so important that people began to think I was important, and I did, too. When the Lord Jesus announced that He would be betrayed, I boasted, 'You can count on me, Lord! I will stand by You! I've bought a sword! If You get into trouble, just call on Peter!' Then a servant girl said to me, 'Don't you belong to Him?' And I said, 'No, I do not!' And a man said, 'Surely you are a Galilean and belong to Jesus!' I denied Him with oaths and cursings." Well, did you fall from grace? "Fall from grace? I fell *into* grace! He put me into the corner, but on the wall He painted His own lambs and sheep and said, 'Peter, lovest thou me? Feed my lambs; feed my sheep.' "

Now, let me ask you: Have you fallen into sin? "Oh yes," you say, "like Abraham, Jacob, Moses, David, Peter, I too played the fool." You know what you have done — things that you blush about when you are all alone, and you say, "Thank God nobody knows about that!" Down in your heart there is some nasty bit of sin — jealousy, envy, strife, lust, cowardice, anger, temper. Did you fall from grace by that? If your particular sin has been confessed, God has restored you; and when God put you into the corner, He went to you there and painted a picture of His forgiveness and love. You learned to fix your eyes more surely upon the Lord Jesus Christ and thus fell into grace — the grace of God. Sin confessed and forsaken has brought many a Christian to fuller knowledge of the grace of God.

When we understand that we do not fall from grace by sinning but that we fall into grace and come closer to God than ever before, we reassess our situation and say:

> Love so amazing, so divine,
> Demands my soul, my life, my all.

"Can I sin against such love?" you ask. Yes, you can. But as we read in 2 Corinthians 5:14, "The love of Christ controls us, because we are convinced that one has died for all; therefore all have died. And he died for all, that those who live might live no longer for themselves but for him who for their sake died and was raised."

Understanding what grace is, we can comprehend that we do not fall from grace by straying into the path of self-will. But am I saying that you can live as you please? Romans 6:1, 2 says, "What shall we say then? Are we to continue in sin that grace may abound? By no means! How can we who died to sin still live in it?" And with utmost horror I turn away from what is called antinomianism — the idea that as long as you believe, you can do as you please. Rather, because of His great love and grace, we seek to live as He wants us to live and to do those things that please Him.

What we do for God is no down payment toward salvation. It is not interest on a debt. Jesus paid it *all*. The love of Christ constrains us to serve Him. Have you ever said to God, "Lord, I love You because you first loved me and sent Your Son to die for me"? If not, do it now, and God will respond by pouring out blessing upon you; He will fill you and thrill you with the knowledge of Himself. Say to Him today, "O God, you sent Jesus Christ to die for me. I thank You and I love You. I want to show that I love You by obeying Your will day by day." That is the fruit of grace.

Chapter Twelve

THE SCALES OF GOD

Among the many Bible passages which teach that salvation is by grace alone, three stand out. The first is Ephesians 2:8,9: "For by grace you have been saved through faith; and this is not your own doing, it is the gift of God — not because of works, lest any man should boast." Next, Titus 3:5 says, "He saved us, not because of deeds done by us in righteousness, but in virtue of his own mercy, by the washing of regeneration and renewal in the Holy Spirit." And last, the verse that I believe is the greatest in the Bible — Romans 4:5: "And to one who does not work but trusts him who justifies the ungodly, his faith is reckoned as righteousness."

When men read these great categorical statements of the nothingness of man's effort, they protest, "Surely God must take some account of what I do!" And God replies, "Turn away from man in whose nostrils is breath, for of what account is he?" (Isa. 2:22).

When I was a small boy in California we spent our summers in Mount Hermon. For supplies we went to a little country store in Felton. In those days there were no electric scales; bread was neither sliced nor wrapped; and you did not buy sugar by weight — you got

a dollar's worth. The grocer scooped sugar from a barrel into a bag
on one side of the scale while he placed weights on the other. Finally
came that magic moment when there was just enough to balance
the scales; then he dropped his scoop into the sugar barrel. Now
the question is, How many pounds of sugar did we get for our dollar?

Someone may say, "I think there were twelve pounds, because I
once read in a book that at that time they sold twelve pounds of
sugar for a dollar." Someone else says, "No, I think there were
thirteen. I used to visit my aunt who had a grocery store in Vermont,
and I personally weighed out thirteen pounds." And a third person
says, "Well, my father told me that his father told him that his father
told him — and it's a strong family tradition — that there were twelve
and one-half pounds for a dollar!"

You see, one person is arguing on the basis of what he has read;
another, on human experience; and the third on family tradition.
But I tell them, "That grocer in the Felton country store put fourteen
pounds of weights on the scales — two five-pound weights, one two-
pound, and two one-pound weights. So for a dollar we got fourteen
pounds of sugar." Only a fool will argue against accurate scales.

Let us apply this story to spiritual life. God says that He has a
scale, and in the Bible He reveals what He has put on His side.
What has God set on His side of the scale? Perfection! God cannot
admit anyone to heaven who is not perfect. "But," says someone,
"nobody is perfect. I'll just abandon that point of view; it is too
theological for me. I shall work up as many ounces as I can: I'll
do the best I can, and hope I get to heaven." That, my friend, is
the surest way *not to get* to heaven.

In the Sermon on the Mount the Lord Jesus said, "You . . . must
be perfect, as your heavenly Father is perfect" (Matt. 5:48). This
was not spoken as a guide to holiness but as a condemnation. The
Sermon on the Mount is the greatest condemnation of man that has
ever fallen from the lips of God. When a man says, "My religion is
the Sermon on the Mount," he reveals his ignorance of the meaning
of that great discourse; he is ignorant of its demands and ignorant of
the fact that it is not a code to live by but a sword that pierces human
pride. The Lord Jesus began the Sermon by saying, "Blessed are the

poor in spirit" — the spiritually bankrupt; and the requirement which you must face and which you cannot meet is the perfection of God.

There are three kinds of people — the very bad, the ordinary, and the very good. Let us weigh these in God's scale. Recalling that there is honor among thieves, let us weigh a thief in the scale. We find that he has only two ounces against God's sixteen. So we take all the people of the criminal class and put them into a heap and write over them the word "Lost."

Now we weigh the average man. He is good enough to keep out of jail, bad enough to do whatever he wants to do, and smart enough to think he can get away with it. This man weighs eight ounces; so he says, "Marvelous! I am four times as good as that convict!" "But," I say, "you are not weighed against the convict, you are weighed against God's sixteen-ounce perfection." And the man says, "Don't be theological. You have just admitted that I am four times as good as that thief!" Nevertheless, eight ounces cannot balance sixteen; so we put this eight-ounce man and all others in his class in the same heap with the two-ounce people — and what a muttering goes on!

Now we come to Judge So and So — an upright, honorable man, beloved in the community, whose heart is open for all good causes; but he does not believe on the Lord Jesus Christ. Set him on the scale; he reaches twelve ounces, the best that the human race can produce. An honest man, the noblest work of God! But the pesky theologian says, "Wait a minute! You are not measured by the eight-ounce man or the two-ounce man; you are being weighed against God's sixteen ounces of perfection. You must admit, Judge, that if all these people were taken to heaven just as they are, it wouldn't be heaven any more." So we set the Judge and all the fine, honorable people of his class on the same heap with the two-ounce and eight-ounce people — and that muttering you heard before was nothing compared with the cries of protest that come from this group.

Alexander Whyte, the great Scotch preacher, once said, "The righteousness of God is that righteousness which His righteousness requires Him to require." When we sift that out, it means that God is so holy that He must demand of us holiness and righteousness equal to His own. For if He permitted anything less, He would be accepting imperfection and heaven would be less than perfect. But you say,

"Do you mean that my righteousness is no better in God's sight than the righteousness of a criminal?" Beyond question, that is exactly what the Bible teaches. The only kind of righteousness that God will accept is divine righteousness, perfect righteousness, which He provides as a gift to all who receive Jesus Christ as Savior.

Now, there are many kinds of righteousness which seem good, but are good only for earth, not for heaven. This may be illustrated by an incident which occurred to a friend of mine who does not see well. He entered a New York subway station and found that he needed some change in order to get through the turnstile. The man in the change booth gave him the necessary coins, but to my friend's fingers one coin did not seem quite right. He told the man that he did not believe he had a dime in his hand. The change-maker brusquely brushed him on his way, saying that he knew what he had given in change. My friend put the coin into the turnstile slot, and at once the mechanism became jammed, much to the disgust of the change-booth man. Quite angry by this time, he went to the turnstile, opened the box, and discovered that an American mechanism, geared for American coins, refused to accept the foreign coin which he had given the man who could not see well. Evidently the foreign coin looked like an American one, but the mechanism rejected it because it was not an American coin. Our own righteousness may pass for good coin here on earth, but the only currency that is acceptable in heaven is God's perfect righteousness. Romans 10:3 speaks of people who, "Being ignorant of the righteousness that comes from God, and seeking to establish their own, they did not submit to God's righteousness," and hence remained lost in trespasses and sins.

Into the world of the lost came the Lord Jesus Christ. He found friends among the outcasts and was put to death by the good people. Why did these moral, ethical leaders crucify Him? Because He taught that human goodness can take a man to hell but never to heaven and that we must be born again. Christ taught that salvation was by the free grace of God, apart from anything in man. By that teaching He signed His death warrant.

God does not love us because of anything good in us. He condemns sin in all men, but He gives life in Christ to anyone who will believe on Jesus as Savior. If you will say, "O God, I admit that

I fall short of Your perfect righteousness, that I belong in the heap of those who are lost, that I have been weighed in the balance and found wanting," God will reply, "I love you; I have put your sin on My Son the Lord Jesus Christ. Believe on Him, and I will give you His righteousness."

This is what Paul meant when he wrote, "Now the righteousness of God has been manifested apart from law, although the law and the prophets bear witness to it, the righteousness of God through faith in Jesus Christ for all who believe. For there is no distinction; since all have sinned and fall short of the glory of God, they are justified by his grace as a gift, through the redemption which is in Christ Jesus" (Rom. 3:21-24). Thus, when we receive Jesus Christ as Savior, the scales balance perfectly. The full weight of Christ's perfection, the righteousness of God, is put to our account in the transaction in heaven and all our sins are put under the blood of Jesus Christ.

But someone may ask, "May I not present my righteousness along with that of Jesus Christ?" The answer is found in two lines in the great hymn "Rock of Ages":

> Nothing in my hand I bring,
> Simply to Thy cross I cling.

There is the clue. God will never give you Christ until you empty your hands of all that you have. God says, "Drop what you have and I will give you Christ."

When I landed at Makassar in the Celebes a few years ago, I was met by a little Malay boy who carried a bamboo cage containing tiny monkeys about six inches high — perfect little creatures and very cute. The boy trailed me, saying, "Buy a monkey, Mister? one dollar; buy a monkey, Mister?" I looked at the monkeys and went along while the boy followed, lowering his price as he pleaded, "Buy a monkey, Mister? seventy-five cents!" and finally, "fifty cents!" The missionary who met me at the ship explained that we couldn't take the monkey; I gave the boy a tip and he went away happy. The missionary then told me how those monkeys are caught.

There is a gourd that grows long like a string bean and, upon reaching its full length, begins to swell. When the gourd is in the string-bean stage, a boy ties a cord around half of it so that half does not grow; the other half continues to swell, and thus a narrow-necked bottle is formed. Then the boy cuts off the gourd, hollows it out, drops in a couple of handfuls of rice, and ties the gourd to a tree. The little monkey smells the rice, thrusts in his paw to grab it, but cannot pull the paw out. If he would only drop the rice, he could get away, but while he holds on to the food his paw acts like a cork in reverse and he is a prisoner of his own greed. Then the boy finds the monkey in the trap, and although the animal chatters, pulls and tugs, he still holds on to the rice. The boy slips a bamboo cage around him, then breaks the gourd. The monkey eats the rice and is sold down the river.

That is the picture of many people who have their hands full of sin, full of themselves. God says, "I will give you salvation to take you into heaven if you will admit that you have your paw full of something and if you will drop it. Admit that you are less than perfect, that you are the sinner that I say you are. Unless you open your hand and drop what you are clutching, I cannot give you My righteousness in Jesus Christ."

Oh, if you will but empty your hands of your own goodness, empty your hands of faith in your church membership, in your baptism! Drop everything and come with nothing — come as a spiritual bankrupt! God will give you Christ, for He is satisfied with Christ's righteousness, and He will enable you to balance His demands perfectly in His scale.

Chapter Thirteen

PAID IN FULL

Do you know what it is to get a receipt marked, "Paid in Full"? What a relief to know that your debt is paid! Our Lord Jesus Christ paid in full a debt which neither you nor I nor any other person could ever pay. In Hebrews 10:12 we read, "But this man [Jesus Christ], after he had offered sacrifice for sins for ever, sat down on the right hand of God." The Revised Standard Version renders it: "But when Christ had offered for all time a single sacrifice for sins, he sat down at the right hand of God."

First, the mind of God planned the cross. The death of Jesus Christ was not an afterthought or an accident. It was not like the Battle of the Bulge in World War II, when the Germans launched a surprise attack on the Allied troops at Bastogne and disrupted the time schedule. No angel rushed to the throne of God and said, "Lord, the enemy has broken through left of center and our divisions are in retreat!" No! We can be absolutely certain that He knows the end from the beginning. Nothing has ever happened unless it has first passed through the will of God.

During the First World War, I enlisted in the Aviation Section of the Army Signal Corps. I learned to fly a plane made of wood, held together with wires, covered with cloth, and painted with banana oil. We went up in open cockpits; parachutes were unknown. Those were the days! There were 40 fellows to fly two planes, so 38 of us sat around and watched the flimsy craft. Suddenly, there were only 37, then 36, and then 35. We sat and talked, and when we saw some fellow go up we would say, "Well, what's going to happen to you?" And sometimes he didn't come back. One day someone asked me, "What about you?" I answered, "This I know: since I am a Christian, not a bullet can kill me or an airplane spill me until God permits it." This is the very basis of our Christian faith: God has planned every event of life.

One passage that speaks about God's plan is 1 Peter 1:18-20: "You know that you were ransomed from the futile ways inherited from your fathers, not with perishable things such as silver or gold, but with the precious blood of Christ, like that of a lamb without blemish or spot. He was destined before the foundation of the world but was made manifest at the end of the times for your sake." Now suppose before the foundation of the world an angel had asked, "God, what are You going to do?"

God would reply, "I am going to create the sun, the moon and the stars, and I shall put My Son Jesus to death on a little piece of dust called Earth."

"But You haven't even created Earth, and yet You plan to have Jesus die on it?"

"That is right," God would say.

The Word of God teaches that before God created this earth, He planned that Jesus should become a man and die here. And thus we were redeemed by blood, not by money; it was precious and imperishable and sacrificial. It was according to what was written in the Word of God, according to the eternal plan of God. So 1 Peter 1:18-20 teaches that God planned this once-for-all sacrifice of Jesus Christ.

Second, the law of God demanded the cross. After man sinned, God sent Moses and through him gave the law. We must understand that Moses was not nearly so important as some people think he was. The great character of the Old Testament was Abraham. Moses was relatively unimportant. I like to compare Moses to a present-day employee of the State Highway Department. He has a pickup truck full of signs. He drives along the road and sets out a sign saying, "Thou shalt not cross the yellow line"; another, "School Zone — thou shalt slow down to 15 miles an hour." This was the work of Moses. God did not plan for the human race to be saved by Moses who merely put up signs so that when some people go too fast and God overtakes them, they cannot say, "I did not know." God says, "I put up this sign so you will know what My will is. I don't want you to have other gods before Me; I don't want you to make any graven images. I want you to honor your father and your mother. You shall not kill; you shall not steal; you shall not commit adultery; you shall not bear false witness."

Since God knew that man would break His law, He decreed that there must be payment for guilt; but Galatians 3:13 tells us, "Christ redeemed us from the curse of the law, having become a curse for us — for it is written, 'Cursed be everyone who hangs on a tree.'" So God wrote into His very law that the wages of sin is death, and this is why a lamb was killed every morning and every night. Every sunrise and every sunset saw blood spilled. Why? In order to impress upon the people the thought, "Sin means death!" When we sin, it means our death or the death of the Savior.

Let us face it: my sin, your sin, must be punished by death forever. Death means separation, for that is all death is. When the body dies, it is the separation of the soul and spirit from the body. That is physical death. But the second death is the separation of soul and spirit from God. When a man sins, his soul and spirit have to be put away from God. Men may call it hell, but it means that we shall not see Him because we willfully chose our own way. The worst of all sins is to want our own way.

In the third place, the Word of God promised the cross. I take you to one of the most beautiful stories in the Old Testament, the sacrifice of Isaac in Genesis 22. God had said, "Abraham, your son Isaac, born when you were one hundred years old, is going to live and have children."

"Thank You, Lord," said Abraham.

"Your children will be as the stars of the sky and as the sands of the sea. Do you believe Me?"

"Yes, Lord, I believe You."

"All right," said God. "Take Isaac up on the mountain, tie him to an altar and kill him. Offer him up to Me as a burnt sacrifice."

"Now," said Abraham, "two and two are four. Isaac is not yet married; he is not a father; and God says he is to have children. But now God tells me to kill him. Well, Lord, You have worked Your way into a corner, and You will have to perform a miracle in order to keep from being a liar. Come on, Isaac! We're going to see a miracle!" And off they started for Mount Moriah.

Arriving at the foot of the mountain, they left their pack-animal and Abraham said to the servants, "You stay here. I and the young man will go up the hill and *we shall return*." Thus he announced that *both* were coming down. As they went up, they carried bundles of sticks to build the fire. Isaac said, "But Father, where is the lamb?" Abraham replied, "God will provide himself the lamb for a burnt offering, my son" (Gen. 22:8). And then there is this beautiful verse: "So they went both of them together." I see in this God the Father and God the Son going to Calvary, together. And so Paul tells us that at Calvary, "God was in Christ reconciling the world to himself" (2 Cor. 5:19).

No doubt Abraham explained to Isaac, "My son, God has told me to do this." And Isaac doubtless replied, "It is all right, Father; I love you and I trust you. If God has told you to put me to death, He knows what He is doing." This we infer from the fact that Christ said, "No man takes my life from me. I have power to lay it down and I have power to take it again" (John 10:18). So Abraham tied the boy to the altar and lifted the knife, but God Almighty caught his arm and showed him a ram, caught in the thicket by his horns, and Abraham offered him as a substitute for Isaac. All this was a pageant (Heb. 11:19) as well as a historical incident. God was portraying the gift by the father of his only son. When Abraham cut the cords and Isaac rose from the altar, it was a picture of the Lord Jesus Christ being raised from the dead. Thus in this story we see God the Father and God the Son; and we see Jesus Christ rising from the dead. And as they went down the hill together, I believe there was fulfilled that which Jesus Christ spoke of later in John 8:56: "Abraham saw my day, and was glad."

In the fourth place, note that the cross was demanded by the holiness of God. In Mark 15:34 Jesus cried out, *"Eloi, Eloi, lama sabachthani?"* — "My God, my God, why hast thou forsaken me?" Why did God the Father forsake Jesus Christ? It was so that He would not have to forsake you and me. In His holiness, God was showing that your sin and my sin must be crushed, either in ourselves or put on Jesus Christ and crushed in Him. If in ourselves, it will carry us to hell; if we take Him as our substitute, our sacrifice for sin, we shall go to heaven. The holiness of God demanded that Jesus Christ die on the cross because sin must be crushed and punished.

In the fifth place, the love of God provided the cross. We all know John 3:16 — "For God so *loved* the world, that he gave his only begotten Son, that whosoever believeth in him should not perish, but have everlasting life." This love of God saw that sin must be punished. Was it to be punished in me and in you? Were we to be struck because of our sins? Were all of us to be sent to hell? No man would ever be in heaven if God had not done something about sin. So God said, "I shall strike My Son, and I shall strike Him once for all" — *once,* not twice. Jesus died *once for all.*

In the sixth place, the Son of God accomplished the cross. In John 10 Jesus said, "I am the good shepherd. The good shepherd lays down his life for the sheep. . . . For this reason the Father loves me, because I lay down my life, that I may take it again. No one takes it from me, but I lay it down of my own accord" (vs. 11, 17, 18). No doubt you have heard people talk about the cross of Christ as though Jesus got into a trap and a lot of big fellows gathered around and He could do nothing about it. In John 18 we have the story of the arrest of Jesus Christ in the Garden of Gethsemane. The troops surrounded the mountain and closed in upon Jesus. He faced them and said, "Whom are you looking for?" They replied, "Jesus of Nazareth"; and He said, "I am he." The next verse says, "They fell to the ground."

Years ago I owned a little movie projector which had a lever to stop the movie so that one frame became a still, like a stereopticon slide. When I pushed the lever the other way, it became a movie again. That is what happened in Gethsemane. As the troops approached Jesus and He said, "I am he, they went backward and fell to the ground" (v. 6). And they would be there yet, if Jesus had not allowed them to move. "All right," He said in effect, "now you can take Me and kill Me."

If you had been a doctor standing by the cross when Jesus died and you had been ordered to sign a certificate stating cause of death, what would you have written? "Loss of blood?" Nonsense! Jesus said, "I am the life." You cannot put life to death! The cause of Jesus' death was, "He dismissed His spirit." During those six hours on the cross He offered one sacrifice for sin forever.

In the Bible, the cross of Christ separates all time into "then" and "now." Ephesians 2:13 says, "But *now* in Christ Jesus you who once were far off have been brought near in the blood of Christ." What changed *once* into *now*? The answer is, Christ died! It delights me to know that when a Russian atheist says, "I shall meet you on Sunday," in the Russian language he has to say, "I shall meet you on Resurrection Day."

Now we come to the most important point: Christ accomplished the death, and the justice of God accepted it. God the Judge is in heaven, and Jesus has died. Is God satisfied? Crucifixion day passes, two days; three days pass, and Jesus is raised from the dead. The justice of God says, "Paid in Full!" You and I have a receipt which guarantees that we shall find nobody guarding the gate of heaven. The door is open, and if you believe in the Lord Jesus Christ you are welcome. If some angel should say, "But aren't you a sinner?" you would answer, "Look at this receipt. It is signed with the blood of Christ and it says, 'Paid in Full.'" The justice of God has accepted it.

Finally, the grace of God gives us the cross, makes it personal for us, and its benefits are for us today. Romans 3:24 says we are "justified by his grace as a gift." The King James Version puts it, "Being justified freely . . ."; and the Greek word translated *freely* is found elsewhere in the New Testament, in John 15:25: "They hated me *without a cause.*" And so we are justified without a cause in ourselves.

It is all the grace of God poured out upon us because Christ died for us.

Why did people hate Jesus without a cause? There was no cause in Him; but the cause was in themselves. They wanted to run their own lives. "God, don't try to tell us what to do!" When Jesus said, "This is what God wants," men hated Him and said, "We will not have this man to reign over us. Get out of our way!" and they nailed Him to the cross.

But although the unbeliever is indifferent to the sacrifice of Christ, the believer says, "O God, my sin is so terrible that Jesus had to die for me! Love so amazing, so divine, demands my soul, my life, my all." And God says, "Justification is yours, without a cause."

And thus Jesus Christ loved me without any cause in me. Was there anything in me to cause God to love me? Not a thing. Why did You love me, O God? And God replies, "Don't look within yourself to find the reason." You may look from one end of life to the other for the reason why God loves you, but you will end only by accepting it as a wonderful, unexplainable fact. Never forget that God loves you! He loves you! Why? Because God is love.

So Hebrews 10:12 teaches us that Christ died once for all; the cross of Jesus Christ was once for all. The mind of God planned it; the law of God demanded it; the Word of God promised it; the holiness of God required it; the love of God provided it; the Son of God accomplished it; the justice of God accepted it; and the grace of God gave it to me and to you without a cause, freely, once for all.

Oh, thank God, our debt of sin is "Paid in Full!"

Chapter Fourteen

GOD'S COMMAND TO BELIEVE

Army discipline is serious! A private does what the sergeant orders him to do. The sergeant takes orders from a second lieutenant. All the way through the military ranks there is order and discipline, established in a way that fixes responsibility and brings unity of command. Suppose, however, that a private is standing near his quarters when an officer passes by. The officer notices something that needs to be cleaned up and orders the private to take care of it. What if the soldier should reply, "Now, Colonel, can't we talk this over? I think the matter should be done this way. . . ." About that time the private would find himself in the guardhouse. It is the soldier's duty to obey, instantly and without question.

The same principle is presented in the Bible. God has authority over every one of His creatures, and all the wrong and misery in this world today are directly traceable to the fact that man is a rebel against God. The story of man's temptation and fall in the Garden of Eden is not only absolute fact but a picture of the rebellion of the entire human race. Thus Paul wrote to the Ephesians, "You once walked following the course of this world, following the prince of

the power of the air, the spirit that is now at work in the sons of
disobedience" (2:2). And because human beings are sons of disobedience, God gives them a still more terrible name in the next
verse — "children of wrath."

Scripture tells us that Adam deliberately and definitely chose to
rebel against God, for we read of him in 1 Timothy 2:14, "Adam was
not deceived." He knew God's command against eating the fruit;
he was not led astray by the promises of Satan; he exalted his own
will above the perfect will of his Creator. On the other hand, the
same verse tells us, "The woman was deceived." Eve thought she
was doing the right thing. She believed that her course of action
would improve the status of her husband and that they would become
like gods through knowing good and evil. For this reason, the woman
is never blamed in the Bible; the blame is put entirely upon the man.
Humorists may joke about the old theme of Mother Eve getting us
all into trouble by eating the forbidden fruit, but the Bible tells us
differently. We read in Romans:

"Therefore as sin came into the world through one man and death
through sin, and so death spread to all men because all men sinned. . .
many died through one man's trespass . . . because of one man's
trespass, death reigned through that one man. . . . Then as one
man's trespass led to condemnation for all men . . . by one man's
disobedience many were made sinners" (Rom. 5:12-19).

And I Corinthians tells us that "in Adam all die" (15:22).

All these passages teach that sin came into the world because of
the rebellion and disobedience of one man, Adam.

As in the early days of man's history on earth, so today, God has a
definite commandment. The thunder of the law on Sinai was the
result of the lightning of His perfect righteousness: "Thou shalt . . .
thou shalt not." It revealed the righteousness of God which no man
can duplicate. It was all summed up by Moses and quoted by Christ:
"Hear, O Israel: The Lord our God is one Lord; and you shall love
the Lord your God with all your heart, and with all your soul, and
with all your might" (Deut. 6:4, 5). These words Moses commended
Israel to write on the heart. The people were to teach them to their
children, to talk of them when sitting at home, and when walking
along the road. They were to be talked about when people were lying

down and when they were sitting up; they were to be bound upon the hand, and put upon the doorposts of the houses.

This law was a summary of the righteousness of God. He knew that no man would ever be able to live up to that standard of perfection; nevertheless, He commanded men to obey the law. Why did God give commands which He knew were impossible for men to fulfill? Because His very holiness could accept nothing less.

However, at the same time God gave the law, He gave the lamb. He directed Moses to speak these words which carried a curse and a condemnation; and he directed Aaron to take a lamb and shed its blood upon the altar for the sins of Israel. The religion of the Jews was originally built upon these two simple facts: God commanded the impossible through Moses, and God did the impossible through Aaron. The great tragedy of the Old Testament is that the people did not understand this balance between the law of God and His grace. They forgot the grace of God and attempted to accomplish the impossible. The result was that they whittled down the demands of God to fit their own failures and soon they were living upon a level which not only failed to satisfy God but brought His curse upon them.

The sufferings of Israel throughout history come not from the fact that the Pharisees delivered Christ to the Roman authorities to be crucified. We confess with shame that Jews have been persecuted in the name of Christ by those who call themselves Christians but who certainly were not living up to Christ's standards. True Christians, however, have long apologized to Israel for every such persecution. Nevertheless, Israel broke the covenant which her fathers made with God more than 1400 years before the Lord Jesus Christ was born. The flights and terrors of Israel were plainly described and foretold in the Book of Deuteronomy and in the prophecies of Isaiah, Jeremiah, Ezekiel and other prophets.

The position of Israel is summed up in the passionate cry of Paul the Jew who wrote, "Brethren, my heart's desire and prayer to God for Israel is, that they might be saved. For I bear them record that they have a zeal of God, but not according to knowledge. For they being ignorant of God's righteousness, and going about to establish their own righteousness, have not submitted themselves unto the righteousness of God. For Christ is the end of the law for right-eousness to every one that believeth" (Rom. 10:1-4).

But what of the Gentile? Is his position before God better than that of the Jew? No, indeed! Be he Mohammedan, Buddhist, or what you will; a worshipper of demons in the jungles of Africa or a worshipper of himself on Park Avenue, he is responsible to obey the command of God and liable to the discipline that will fall upon him as he practices unrighteousness. To have heard about the Bible or never to have heard of it is beside the question, for we read: "The wrath of God is revealed from heaven against all ungodliness and wickedness of men who by their wickedness suppress the truth. For what can be known about God is plain to them, because God has shown it to them. Ever since the creation of the world his invisible nature, namely, his eternal power and deity, has been clearly per-ceived in the things that have been made. So they are without excuse" (Rom. 1:18-20).

Who is without excuse? The uncivilized man and the civilized man. The Indian in the Amazon jungle should look at the stars, watch the flow of the river ever beating toward the sea, study the tapering curve of the fish that he spears, the color of the sunset, the plumage of the tropical birds. When he sees these things, what should the savage do? He should fall prostrate before the Creator who is revealed in this creation. He should cry out, "O mighty Being, I confess Thy perfection! I throw myself upon Thy mercy! I recognize my own nothingness! I confess that I have lived without thought of Thee, and I deserve the wrath which must come from Thee because of my unrighteousness!" We may be sure that the same Lord who heeded the cry of the Gentile woman who said, "Yes, Lord, yet even the dogs eat the crumbs that fall from their master's table" (Matt. 15:27), that same Lord, I say, would give to the savage the knowledge of His salvation and grace. He would send His light into that darkened soul. But the savage goes on in rebellion, building altars to demon gods and giving himself over to all sorts of unclean-ness and lasciviousness.

The case of the civilized man is not much different. He has blotted out the stars with city lights until they are but pale points above his towers, which, he likes to think, scrape the sky. But although he has forgotten the stars, God still sends down their light through the telescopes of astronomers that man may learn of a universe that staggers the imagination. Civilized man has forgotten the God who made the power in the rivers which sweep past his cities. But God has given man the intelligence to dam those rivers, transform their power and send it along wires to light cities, speed trains, clean homes, open doors, and furnish a thousand willing slaves to do his work. Man has stirred the dirt of his cities into a dusty haze that hides the glory of the sunset, but God has put color into the eyes of genius so that our museums are filled with Rembrandts, Leonardos, and Holbeins. God put harmony into the deaf ears of Beethoven and the keen ears of Ormandy, agility into the fingers of the artists of piano and orchestra, which combine to give us a faint idea of the beauties and glories of heaven.

What should the civilized man do when he sees and hears these wonders round about him? He should fall prostrate before the Creator who is thus revealed, and he should say, "O mighty Being, I confess Thy perfection, and I throw myself upon Thy mercy. I recognize my own nothingness. I confess that I have lived my life without thought of Thee, and I deserve the wrath which must come upon my unrighteousness. Deal with me in Thy grace and loving-kindness." To such a man God could respond in the words of John 3:16: "God so loved the world that he gave his only Son, that whoever believes in him should not perish but have eternal life." We may be sure that God would give to such a man the knowledge of His salvation and grace, and He would send His light into that darkened soul.

But civilized man does not behave in that way. All the symphonies of light, power, color, harmony and other glories of life do not turn his heart from self-will and self-worship. He continues to worship the creature and the creation more than the Creator; thus he brings upon himself the condemnation of God and the divine declaration that he is without excuse!

But this God who has commanded men to be righteous and to do righteously would be an arbitrary monster if He left them helpless to be and do what He demands. The glory of the Christian message lies in the fact that God makes a free offer of life and power to those whom He has declared incapable of meeting His demands. He has examined the resources of man and has declared him spiritually bank-rupt. But God has promised to pay all man's debts and provide him with a new capital stock of righteousness. This is the heart of what God calls the gospel, or the good news of salvation. In the passage from the tenth chapter of Romans there was the statement of man's insolvency: "Being ignorant of the righteousness that comes from God, and seeking to establish their own, they did not submit to God's righteousness." But immediately there follows the statement of the way of salvation: "Christ is the end of the law, that every one who has faith may be justified" or made righteous (Rom. 10: 3, 4).

In other words, we are to look to the incarnation of the Lord Jesus Christ and the work which He accomplished in presenting Himself as our Savior. This work was done not so much to satisfy man as to satisfy the nature of God. In thinking about God certain laws are to be observed, just as in working with electricity. Electricity can be man's great friend if its laws are observed. Insulation, direc-tion, quantity control, and many other laws of electricity demand perfect obedience or we shall suffer consequences of destroyed fuses, burned buildings or stopped hearts. Why will men refuse to see that it is exactly the same with God? He must work according to His nature. If men will submit to the righteousness of God as re-vealed in the Lord Jesus Christ, they may enjoy all the blessings that accompany that righteousness; but if men refuse to submit to the righteousness of God, they must suffer the condemnation that flows from that righteousness. Just as electricity says in effect, "You may have light and power, or you may have a thunderbolt," so God says, "You may have spiritual light and power, or you shall have the divine thunderbolt."

The Word of God reveals that He has issued divine commands for men to believe in Him. Many people are so accustomed to hearing the gospel spoken of as a divine invitation that they overlook the fact that faith and obedience are commanded by God. With this thought in mind, I have gone over the New Testament, and have been amazed to find many verses ordinarily considered invitations, which may also be read as absolute commands. At the close of His public ministry the Lord Jesus declared, "He who rejects me and does not receive my sayings has a judge; the word that I have spoken will be his judge on the last day. For I have not spoken on my own authority; the Father who sent me has himself given me commandment what to say and what to speak. And I know that his commandment is eternal life" (John 12:48-50). After meditating on this passage, I saw that most of the gospel invitations could be given in a tone of command; for example, "Come to me, and I will give you rest" (Matt. 11:28). "O taste and see that the Lord is good" (Ps. 34:8) is the voice of the doctor ordering a new diet. "Hear and your soul shall live" (Isa. 55:3) is an order that tunes out mental static and get us on God's wave length. "Follow me," is the command of the superior officer to leave not only the nets which need mending but all the nets in which you have been caught.

On Mars Hill in Athens, the Apostle Paul gave this command to the Gentile world, after viewing the idol worship into which men had sunk: "We ought not to think that the Deity is like gold, or silver, or stone, a representation by the art and imagination of man. The times of ignorance God overlooked, but now he commands all men everywhere to repent, because he has fixed a day on which he will judge the world in righteousness by a man whom he has appointed, and of this he has given assurance to all men by raising him from the dead" (Acts 17:29-31).

Have you heeded that command? It is the last of all the commandments, more important than all the Ten Commandments, for it will give you eternal life, and power to live according to the righteousness of God — which the Ten Commandments can never do. God "commands all men everywhere to repent"; He therefore commands you. Repentance simply means a change of mind. Too long have you had your own mind and done as you please. Now God commands you to change your mind about two things. First, you must give up the idea that you can get along by yourself, that you can satisfy the righteous demands of God, that you can attain a life that will measure up to God's standard. Instead, accept the verdict of God that you are a spiritual bankrupt when measured by His righteousness. Second, you must turn away from your own self-sufficiency and turn to the Lord Jesus Christ. He is the end of the law for righteousness to every one who believes. Accept today God's verdict that He is satisfied with the death of His Son as the propitiation for your sins. Then He will give you divine righteousness through this Savior, Jesus Christ our Lord.

PART FOUR

MARKS OF A SAINT
"Beloved of God, Called Saints"

The fact that we are saints means that we are confronted with the responsibility to walk as the sons of God among the sons of men. This high duty and privilege is ours because, having been planted in His death, we have been raised to newness of life in Him.

Chapter Fifteen

MARKS OF SONSHIP

During the season of Lent, Christendom is busy with its spring house-cleaning. In olden days the early church set aside forty hours for devotion; this period was lengthened to six weeks. The true believers were desirous of glorifying their Lord by a pure life lived wholly unto Him. It was not long, however, before the spirituality of the church was weakened. That which was meant to glorify God degenerated into lifeless formalism. Like a shell without its kernel is Lent without the life. To believers, however, each day of the year, each hour of the day, should be a time of devotion to our Lord. Such a life gives evidence of spiritual growth. In this section of the book I want to set before you the marks of a true saint. I shall begin with the marks of sonship, the evidence that we have become children of God through faith in Jesus Christ our Lord.

The fact that we can call ourselves sons of God is a miracle of God's great love to us. Love that goes upward from the heart of man to God is adoration. Love that goes outward, from one heart to another, is affection. Love that stoops, is grace.

God stooped to us. For us, this is the most stupendous fact of

125

the universe. It reveals to us that our God is love. We cannot find love in the forces of nature. There may be ·plan and determination, order and intelligence, but you cannot find love. There is nothing in the movements of the millions of suns that fleck the universe, nothing within the range of telescope or microscope that indicates love in nature. You cannot put love into a test tube, measure it with a micrometer, synthetize or analyze it. Love is not to be found in the forces of nature.

You think you see it in a calm scene of natural beauty. You stand in the pine forest and listen to the soft sound of the wind in the branches, the whir of a bird's wing. The smell of the sea comes up on the breeze to swell your heart. Then the wind changes, clouds drive forward, the thunder roars, the lightning strikes the trees; hail beats down the flowers; the sea crashes against the shore. Where is the love?

You stroll down the street and your eye catches the warm light coming from a window. You glance into the room. What a scene of comfort! A father sits in a big chair reading; children play on the rug before the fire; the mother sits nearby, sewing. Suddenly she rises and touches one of the little ones on the cheek. She glances at the father and speaks a word. He looks at the child and then telephones for a doctor. The doctor comes, then a nurse, then the undertaker. Where is love in the forces with which we have to contend?

If we had no other evidence, we could never know that God is love. He could alter the stars in their courses and make them into fiery letters across the sky that would spell out the words, "God loves you," — but were there no other evidence than those starry letters we would have a right to let doubt gnaw our hearts and to think that we were the unfortunate playthings of some fortuitous hazard.

But God has demonstrated His love. When we were dead in trespasses and sins, He came — not clinging to the brightness of His glory, not shunning our lowly condition, but taking upon Himself the form of a servant in the likeness of men. And that was not all. "Being found in fashion as a man, he humbled himself, and became obedient unto death, even the death of the cross" (Phil. 2:8). Now I know that God is not some far-distant, impersonal force. Now I know that God is love.

When Christ went to the cross, God saw us hanging there with Him. When He died, God saw us, judicially, dying with Him. When He was raised, we were quickened together with Him. When He ascended into heaven, we were taken with Him and counted as sitting together with Him in the heavenly places. We who were not sons but enemy aliens were brought into the full privilege of sonship. When our time came to live, the Spirit of God told us that we were sinners. Our minds recognized the truth of the accusation. The Spirit of God pointed to the cross of Jesus Christ: our sin placed Him there. Melted by the thought of so much love, we believed God's verdict about the righteousness of Christ, and He placed it to our account. We accepted God's provision for sonship and, marvel of marvels, we passed out of death into life and became His sons.

Do you have that supernatural life within you? Are you certain that you have been born again? Have you looked away to the cross of Jesus Christ and found there the payment for your sin and the provision for your eternal righteousness?

Upon those who have thus believed, God puts the marks of sonship. What are these marks of sonship? What does God expect from those whom He has called to be sons and titled as His heirs?

The first mark of sonship is the right to become a son of God. Many who speak of the Fatherhood of God are either stealing a privilege that they know is not theirs, or they are deceived into believing that they have a privilege which has never been granted them. "But as many as received him, to them gave he power to become the sons of God, even to them that believe on his name" (John 1:12).

Several Greek words are translated by our word *power*. One is *dunamis*, from which we get dynamite and dynamo. It is that power which manifests itself in mighty works. "The gospel of Christ . . . is the *power* of God unto salvation to everyone that believeth" (Rom. 1:16). It is a divinely provided energy which changes lives. Another word is *kratos* from which we get autocrat, plutocrat, aristocrat, democrat. It is the power which manifests itself in dominion and rule. Neither of these words is used in John 1:12. The word here is *exousia*, authority or right. When Jesus overturned the tables of the moneychangers, He was asked, "By what *authority* doest thou these things?" It is the same word. As many as receive Christ, to them God has given the right and authority to become the sons of God, even to them that believe on His name. It is not true that all men are sons of God, but all who believe on the Lord Jesus Christ *become* the sons of God. Thus the first mark of sonship is the right, the authority, to be a son of God and to call Him Father.

What do I say? Call Him Father? Yes, that is the second mark of sonship. We have received the authority to be sons; we receive the right to call Him Father. It was not always so. You do not find any suggestion of this privilege in the Old Testament. Our relationship to God as sons depended upon the work which Christ accomplished at the cross of Calvary.

How different our manner of approach to God from that of believers who lived before Christ came! This fact is not always understood, even by Christians. The following incident illustrates this point. In 1918, just after the Armistice which ended World War I, a great Bible conference was held in Carnegie Hall in New York city. The minister who opened the first session with prayer addressed God in this manner: "O Thou great and terrible God, great is Thy majesty, great is the distance that separates us from Thee! From the abyss of our helpless and lost condition we cry after Thee, guilty sinners that we are! Have mercy upon us, O God. . . ." There was much more in the same vein; but about that moment in the prayer one of the Bible teachers on the platform, a dear old man of God who is now in heaven, whispered softly to the man next him, "Why doesn't someone give that man a New Testament?" We do not need to stand off from God, afraid to approach because of the majesty of His holiness. He has told us that we may come boldly to the throne of grace to find strength for help in time of need. He has preached peace to us who were afar off so that we might draw near with full assurance.

When Christ hung upon the cross, dying in the darkness, there was a great earthquake and the veil of the temple was torn in two from top to bottom. This act disclosed the Holy of Holies to the public eye. Till that moment no man had ever gone behind that veil except the high priest. He went only once a year, on the day of atonement, and never without offering first a sacrifice for his own sins and then a second sacrifice for the sins of the people. Taking the blood of this second sacrifice, he entered the Holy of Holies behind the veil and sprinkled the blood on the mercy seat, the dwelling place of God among His people. This form had been ordained by God in order to teach that He is holy and cannot be approached at will. There is but one way to God, the way that recognizes His holiness and His justice. It is the way of sacrifice. Christ made one sacrifice for sins forever (Heb. 10:12). Nothing now stands between the soul and God — no priesthood, no altar, no sacrifice. All has been swept aside and the way is open for us to come boldly. Christ has died. Ah, yes, the New Testament has done all this for us. No longer do we cry, "O Thou great and terrible God! great is the distance that separates us from Thee!" Rather do we come reverently to the throne and cry, "Abba, Father!"

What does that word *Abba* mean? Some years ago I spent a few months in a small city in the Near East. In the cool of the evening I sat out in the courtyard of the house and listened to the language of the people, trying to catch a word here and there. A woman called one of the children playing nearby, and as he ran toward her I heard him call her "Mama." Then a man came down the street, and a little girl ran to him crying, "Abba!" It was the equivalent of our Papa or Daddy. This is the meaning of Romans 8:15 when we cry, "Abba, Father." God wants us to know Him in the intimacy of father and child.

God broke down barriers between the soul and Himself. He came forth in order that enmity might be slain at the cross. Reconciliation, so far as He is concerned, has been accomplished. We are now reconciled to God by the death of His Son. We believed His Word about it, and He put upon us the new robe of spotless righteousness. He begot in us a new life that is eternal because it is the life of the risen Lord Jesus. We are now children of God. He wants us to come to Him in the intimacy that exists between fathers and children.

There is, of course, none of that flippancy which exists in too many homes today; none of that disrespect which children show toward parents. There is none of the know-it-all spirit that leads to lawlessness. When God tells us to address Him as "Abba, Father," it is

actually His Holy Spirit within us who speaks thus. Such words
do not rise from the human heart. The Holy Spirit alone can call
us to such grandeur.

See a father coming home from the day's work. The children
run to meet him. He takes them in his arms and carries them the
last short distance to the house. The baby toddles ecstatically across
the garden walk to meet him. All together they are in one joyous
embrace. All this is in that word *Abba*.

The child moans restlessly in its bed. Fever has stricken it down.
The father places his hand upon the head and the child whispers
from its parched throat, "Daddy!" All this is in that word *Abba*.

The girl or boy of teen age comes home in shame and humiliation
over misconduct. "I didn't mean to do it, Daddy!" The father's
arms are open and their tears are mingled together. And all that is
to be found in these words, "Abba, Father."

Queen Esther trembled as she stood in the court waiting to approach the king. She did not know whether she would be slain for
her temerity or received because of her loveliness and the kindness
of the king. But she saw the scepter of the king raised, and she was
privileged to come a step closer and make her request. The sinner
comes to God through Christ and is received, not as some oriental
potentate might receive one of his court according to the whim of
the moment, but rather on the well-grounded relationship of child to
father.

Abba? Here is what it means. Do you see the handsome man of
fifty meet that splendid youngster of twenty-two who has just been
voted the best all-around man in his class? The father grips the
boy's arm and feels the biceps flex beneath his touch. Strong glance
meets strong glance. "Fine work, Son," says the father. "Forget it,
Dad," says the boy. Their glances meet again. They have recognized
that there is something new between them. The boy is admitted to
a new place in the mind of the father. He has come into the ranks of
manhood. Do you catch what I am getting at? All the loving understanding of this scene is hidden in the word *Abba,* Father.

O God! Abba, Father, God! Our fevered hearts repeat Thy name!
Our sinful, prodigal souls grope their way back to Thee, to find Thee
ever waiting with the robe, the ring and the kiss. The strongest ef-

forts of our yielded spirits, building on Thy Word and on Thy strength, turn back all the glory and the praise to Thee. Abba, Father! The spirit of adoption has engendered that cry within our hearts and formed it on our lips.

Thou dost seek true worshipers? Find in us, children of Thy new creation, that which Thy Father-heart desires, and by our lives yielded up to Thy leading, may we be ever to the praise of the glory of Thy grace.

Chapter Sixteen

MARKS OF THE CHRISTIAN WALK

The way a man walks reveals his personality and character. The words which describe various gaits emphasize this fact; such words as: amble, stroll, slouch, shuffle, stride, prowl; brisk, smart, erect, hesitating, lagging, swift, sure. Since the Bible is a supreme literary masterpiece, as well as spirit and life, it is not surprising to find the life of the believer described as a walk. Let us consider the walk of the Christian in four aspects.

Before anyone can walk, he must be on his feet; and the Christian life cannot be lived until one is a Christian. Although it is self-evident that a baby cannot walk until he has been born, yet people attempt to walk the Christian way before they have been born again. The Bible states categorically that life begins with the new birth and there is no life apart from the redemptive work of the Lord Jesus Christ. If these words should be read by someone who has not been born again, consider the teaching of the Word of God on this point.

There are two classes of non-Christians: those who simply lie down in sin and make no pretense of walking, and those whose walk is ethical and who, therefore, think it is Christian. The Christian life does not rise from efforts to live like Christ, to pattern life by His. That would be like expecting a cigarette butt to shine like the sun. Rather, the Christian life is the outflowing of the presence of Christ, born into the life of the believer at regeneration through the implanting of the divine nature by God.

There can be no Christian life in anyone who is not a Christian. "If any man have not the Spirit of Christ, he is none of his" (Rom. 8:9). This verse is frequently misquoted and misapplied, as though no one belonged to Christ unless he were Christlike. No true believer is Christlike at the beginning of his Christian life. Little by little, day by day, we grow into the measure of the stature of the fullness of Christ; it is a lifelong process, and at the end there is still a vast gap that must be bridged by the transforming power of Christ in our glorification together with Him. The true meaning of the phrase, "If any man have not the Spirit of Christ, he is none of his," lies rather in the presence of divine life, the germ from which Christlikeness may develop.

An electric bulb may be screwed into the socket and the current turned on, but if there is no filament within the bulb there will be no light. So a person may profess to be a Christian, but only by the miracle of the new birth, the creation within him of new life, can the light of Christ shine. Some obstruction may lessen the current so that there is but a tiny glow on the filament, but it is capable of lighting up with full power when unobstructed. The indwelling presence of the Lord Jesus Christ makes one a Christian, and the Bible teaches that comparatively few out of the world's population possess this divine life. To the lost, then, we say, cease to hope in yourself; trust utterly and absolutely in Christ and His death as the propitiation for your sin, and you will be saved.

To one who possesses the life of Christ, the Bible speaks of development under the figure of the Christian walk. In this connection there are four prepositions. To Abram, God said, "I am the Almighty God; walk before me" (Gen. 17:1). Through Moses God commanded the children of Israel, "Ye shall walk after the Lord your God" (Deut. 13:4). Of Enoch and Noah it is written that they walked with God (Gen. 5:24; 6:9). Finally, in the New Testament, we read, "As ye have therefore received Christ Jesus the Lord, so walk ye in him"

(Col. 2:6). Walk *before* the Lord, *after* the Lord, *with* the Lord and *in* the Lord.

First, we are to walk *before* the Lord. Many of us can remember incidents of childhood when we walked before our parents. On our walk to Sunday school I skipped along the sidewalk, stopping to examine a place in the cement where a group of children had left the prints of their hands and bare feet when it was wet and where a horseshoe had been imbedded. At a certain place I would run far ahead and wait at the curb for my father to come up so that I might cross with him. There was one yard where I paused and waited for my father so that he would be near when we passed a huge, barking dog. Walking before my father was a place of absolute safety. His eye was ever upon me, and his voice called out if I strayed.

Certainly it is so with our heavenly Father. He has planned for us to walk before Him in the path of great security. "He knoweth the way that I take" (Job 23:10). We need never fear when our heavenly Father is behind us. He started us on this walk, and He expects to bring us home. Jeremiah heard the Lord say, "For I know the plans I have for you, . . . plans for welfare and not for evil, to give you a future and a hope" (Jer. 29:11). Surely this is in the heart of the Father.

But walking before the Father also means training and discipline. I have seen a father and his children taking a walk in the midst of the big city. There were perils of traffic and other dangers on every hand. The training went on day by day. The children walked before their father and were allowed to run to a certain tree some fifty yards ahead. If they ran beyond it, they had to walk just five steps ahead of the father for many sedate minutes while they fretted for liberty. Upon their promise that they would observe his limits, they were free again. Up to the fixed goal they ran, and stood with their toes to a line, little soldiers obeying with precision. When they had been trained so well that they never overshot their prescribed limit, the distance was raised until they advanced one hundred yards and more. Finally they were released at a certain point and told that they could disappear around the corner and stop at a certain known goal. When that lesson had been learned, they were permitted to cross a quiet street where there was little traffic. When such a crossing had been successfully negotiated on many successive days, they were permitted to cross at a busier corner. Time was passing. Where three-year-olds were halted at fifty yards, and four-year-olds permitted to go around a corner and out of sight, five-year-olds were crossing streets.

One day the father sent the boys ahead where they would cross two streets, gave them money to go into a familiar store and make a purchase, and wait there for him. Distances were lengthened, sums of money were increased, errands were made more important. Finally one day a ten-dollar bill was given to them and they were sent to a bank three or four blocks away to get change and bring it home. Faithful in a few things, they became faithful in many. This is the desire of the father-heart. This is why the heavenly Father tells His children to walk before Him. He desires their growth, their discipline, their training, that they may be strong in the powers that He has given them.

In the second place, we are told that we are to walk *after* the Lord. *2.* We learn to follow our God, shaping our lives by His blessed example. It is quite natural for a boy to wish to be like his earthly father, and it is an unhappy man who so lives that his boy sees flaws that turn him away from following his father. Still more unhappy is the father who so lives as to drag his boy down to his own level of sin.

I once heard of an instance which taught a man that he must be very careful of his life because he was the ideal and example for his son. The father had been making the rounds of several houses on Christmas afternoon and had partaken of various brands of cheer which caused him to walk a crooked path in the snow as he made his way across a field toward home. Finally he heard the voice of his five-year-old calling out behind him. He turned and saw the boy taking great steps in order to put his feet into the tracks left by his father. With a smile the boy said, "See, Daddy, I'm walking right in your footsteps!" The father was sobered as he saw how wavering his track was and resolved at once to mend his ways and be more careful how he walked if his son were to walk after him.

When we walk after the steps of our Lord, we need have no fear, for He is the perfect example. Again let me stress that the unbeliever must not think that he can walk in the path of the Lord, for the non-Christian is dead in trespasses and sins. Only the believer can look to the Lord's life as an example of his walk. "Christ suffered for us, leaving us an example, that ye should follow his steps" (1 Pet. 2:21).

> Trying to walk in the steps of the Saviour,
>   Trying to follow our Saviour and King;
> Shaping our lives by His blessed example,
>   Happy, how happy, the songs that we bring.
>
> How beautiful to walk in the steps of the Saviour,
>   Stepping in the light, stepping in the light,
> How beautiful to walk in the steps of the Saviour,
>   Led in paths of light.

There may well be the ideal of following Christ in our daily living inherent in such a suggestion of walking after Him. But the context of the verse in 1 Peter contains the sobering thought that to follow in the steps of Christ is to follow in His sufferings, and Christ clearly indicated what following Him would mean: "If the world hate you," He said, "ye know that it hated me before it hated you. If ye were of the world, the world would love his own: but because ye are not of the world, but I have chosen you [elected you] out of the world, *therefore* the world hateth you. Remember the word that I said unto you, The servant is not greater than his lord" (John 15:18-20).

Walking after the Lord is the true explanation of what it means to take up our cross and follow Him. There is a common misconception of bearing a cross. For example, a mother once told me that she had a very heavy cross to bear: her son was in prison. That was not a cross, that was a personal tragedy. Another woman said that her cross was a cancer. That was not a cross, that was disease. The only cross in the Bible is the cross of Jesus Christ. When the believer is told to deny self, take up his cross daily, and follow Christ (Luke 9:23), what does this mean? He must count himself as crucified with Christ (Gal. 2:20); he must continually yield his old nature to the Holy Spirit for crucifixion (Rom. 8:13). In taking up the cross, he is taking up likeness to Christ's sufferings. When Christ was reviled, He reviled not again; when He suffered, He threatened not, but committed Himself unto Him who judges righteously (1 Pet. 2:23). To this life we were called, and it is specifically stated that for this type of life Christ set the example and that we are to follow His steps.

With all the sufferings of the Christian life there are pre-eminent compensations. If we walk before the Lord to learn and follow after Him in His sufferings, we have the privilege of walking *with* Him in fruitful companionship. There is an oft-quoted verse in the Book of Amos that needs to be brought up to date. The older version reads, "Can two walk together, except they be agreed?" (3:3). There have been many walks in disagreement; the passage means, "except they be agreed as to where they shall meet to begin walking." The revision reads, "Do two walk together, unless they have made an agreement?" If one person says, "We will meet at the seashore," and the other says, "We will meet in the city," there will be no walk. He tells us that the rendezvous for our walk together begins at the cross of Jesus Christ. To walk with our Lord, we must put down our wills in order to accept His will fully.

Only two men, out of all the Bible, are said to have walked with God: Enoch and Noah. These men lived in an age of apostasy and moral decline that has had no parallel in subsequent history; it will be equaled only in the period immediately preceding the return of the Lord Jesus Christ. "As it was in the days of Noah, so shall it be also in the days of the Son of man" (Luke 17:26). Enoch had this testimony, that he pleased God (Heb. 11:5); and Noah found grace in the eyes of the Lord (Gen. 6:8). Beyond any doubt the characteristic in the lives of these two men that won such praise from God was their willingness to oppose the godlessness of their generation and to warn men that the judgment of God would destroy them.

In the one brief sentence which remains of Enoch's preaching, he repeated the word "ungodly" four times. The burden of his sermon was the ungodliness of the world about him. "Behold, the Lord cometh," he warned his contemporaries, "with ten thousands of his saints, To execute judgment upon all, and to convince all that are ungodly among them of all their ungodly deeds which they have ungodly committed, and of all their hard speeches which ungodly

sinners have spoken against him" (Jude 14, 15). What gave Enoch
and Noah the courage to defy their generation? They walked with
God.

Walking with God is fellowship and companionship; it is also
surrender to His will and agreement with Him. The man who follows Christ accepts the holiness of the Lord as the supreme standard
of living and bows to the sovereignty of God. There can be no fellowship without acknowledgment of the Lord's sovereign right to
do as He pleases and when He pleases; of the Lord's wisdom and
knowledge overruling man's and Satan's devices; and of the Lord's
authority in the believer's own life, to will and to do His good pleasure (Phil. 2:13). The man who walks with God will know Him
as Lord and Master, as sovereign in history and circumstance.

Finally, we are told, "As ye have therefore received Christ Jesus
the Lord, so walk ye in him." This is the climax of our walk. To
walk *in* Christ is to recognize the wealth of our position in Him and
to see our lives as hid with Christ in God (Col. 3:3). The little
word *in* is one of the most potent in the New Testament. If the
epistles are read with care it will be discovered that this preposition
appears coupled with a name of Christ or a pronoun of that name in
a great many instances. "If any man be *in* Christ, he is a new
creature" (2 Cor. 5:17); we are "accepted *in* the beloved" (Eph. 1:6);
"*in* whom we have redemption through his blood" (Eph. 1:7); and
we are "blessed . . . with all spiritual blessings in heavenly places *in*
Christ" (Eph. 1:3). These and many similar passages speak of the
position of the believer as identified with Christ.

There is a profound meaning back of all these uses of this little
word. How did we get to be "in Christ"? The Bible clearly teaches
that this placing of the believer *in* Christ is that work of the Holy
Spirit called the baptism of the Holy Spirit; or more correctly translated, it is the identification of the believer through the Holy Spirit
and the placing of the believer *in* Christ.

We are all familiar with the simple truth of the gospel, that our
salvation is secure because God saw us *in* Christ when our Lord
suffered upon the cross. We are aware of the call to holy living on
the ground that we are counted as being already seated *in* the heavens
with Christ (Eph. 2:6). All these phases of truth are summed up

in the obligation that is ours because of our glorious position *in* Christ.

We have been trained to walk *before* Him. We are called to look upon His sufferings and to be willing to walk *after* Him. He takes us into His closest fellowship and bids us walk *with* Him. All of this obliges us to bring every thought and action into subjection to Christ. Every phase of our life is to be lived within the position that is ours by His death, resurrection and ascension. We are *in* Christ. We have received all this by grace. So let us walk in Him, glorifying Him in our body and in our spirit, which are God's (1 Cor. 6:20).

May the Lord give us grace, day by day, to walk before Him, after Him, with Him and in Him.

Chapter Seventeen

MARKS OF TRUE CONFESSION

One of the great doctrines of the Word of God is the doctrine of confession. Because it has been abused by some churches, its truth has been overlooked by others. In some churches it has been made a substitute for salvation; in others, it has been neglected as a means of Christian growth.

There are those who are very conscious of confession without knowing its true significance. They speak of "going to confession," before they will be permitted to take communion. For them, confession is made by telling a member of the clergy what they have done wrong; but, judging by the lives they live, many such people have no thought of changing their conduct. On the other hand, some people who are saved by the grace of God often display an indifference to the need to confess sins, even to the point where grace, instead of promoting a holy life. almost becomes license for a sinful one.

There is no spiritual merit in confessing our sins to any man, since no man has power to forgive sins but Jesus Christ Himself. But there is great urgency for the true believer to confess his sins to Jesus Christ our Lord, if he is to know moment-by-moment fellowship with God our heavenly Father.

140

There is a great psychological basis for confession. Everyone would
share his burden with someone else. Almost every language carries
the proverb, "A burden shared is a burden halved." In many of his
novels, Dostoevsky shows how his characters, driven by guilt, have
no peace until confession is made. The psychologists speak of this
as a catharsis which gives the soul opportunity for cleansing. People
like to talk out their problems. In fact, some people advertise in the
newspapers, offering to listen to others talk for so much money an
hour. Ministers have had this experience: a person comes to him,
talks for an hour without giving the minister a chance to say a word,
and closes the conversation by saying, "You do not know how much
you have helped me!"

Thus we see that confession is a natural thing. People must un-
burden themselves. But is confession a spiritual benefit to everyone?
The Bible teaches that true confession is for those who have been redeemed, whose sinful natures have been dealt with at the cross through
the death of Christ. It is on the basis of forgiven *sin* that God can
deal with *sins*.

We must pause at this point in order to set forth the doctrine of
salvation in relation to the doctrine of sanctification; or to use more
popular language, we must show the necessity of being born again
before one may live the life of the believer. According to the Word
of God, men are sinners. They are sinners by nature, by choice and
by God's declaration. As a result of their sin they are a total ruin.
By sin, we mean coming short of the perfection of God. "For all
have sinned, and come short of the glory of God" (Rom. 3:23). It
is not a question of what I have done that makes me a sinner; it
is the fact that I have not lived up to the standard which God has
set — His glory. A sinner is anyone who has less than the moral
perfection of God. This makes it impossible for me to be acceptable
to God. By nature I contaminate everything I touch. We are like a
water glass which has been smeared with a culture of smallpox. Into
the glass may be poured distilled water or perhaps spring water. We
offer someone a drink. He refuses because he is suspicious of the
glass. There is no point in analyzing the water when its pollution is
certain. There is no point in quibbling about the nature and degree
of sins if our sinful nature has not been dealt with. All our "good

works" will be tainted by our sinful nature. Whether we have spring water, distilled water, or ditch water, each in turn is infected by the glass. Whether one is a good moral person, a religious person, or a criminal, each is infected by the sinful nature which he possesses.

Man is completely and absolutely ruined by sin. There is only one remedy: the new birth. Through faith in the Lord Jesus Christ, a man is born again, cleansed from his sin, and given new life — the very life of God. Christ becomes the foundation of his life and he is delivered from the power of sin. Men are lost because all died in Adam, and the question we must ask of every man is, "Are you born again?" We are not to be concerned with the number and character of men's sins — all men must be born again, all must step upon the true Foundation which is Jesus Christ.

In wonderful grace God took care of sin once and for all, judicially settling the account by the death of Jesus Christ. Our sin was charged against Him and His righteousness was credited to us. Now we are forgiven, made righteous, welcomed to the Father's presence. The true believer possesses a peace with God which nothing can ever take away.

Apart from salvation in Christ, the root of man's sin can never be reached. Dealing with it piecemeal never solves the problem. No sacrament, no ritual, no religious formula can reach the root. Christ has made peace by the blood of His cross, and there is no other means to peace with God. Confession without salvation is but the application of a salve; one may chase boils from one place to another on the spiritual frame without cleansing the poison from the blood stream. Confession does not redeem man; only the blood of Christ can do that.

We come now to the Biblical doctrine of confession. John tells us, "If we confess our sins, he is faithful and just to forgive us our sins, and to cleanse us from all unrighteousness" (1 John 1:9). If we confess . . . John is addressing believers, for he says in the next chapter, "My little children, I am writing this to you so that you may not sin; but if any one does sin, we have an advocate with the Father, Jesus Christ the righteous; and he is the expiation for our sins, and not for ours only but also for the sins of the whole world" (2:1, 2).

Thus born-again believers have Jesus Christ as Advocate and Sacrifice acceptable to God.

Again, in 1 John 5:13 we read, "I write this to you who believe in the name of the Son of God, that you may know that you have eternal life." Thus we in 1 John 1:9 are those who are trusting Christ for eternal life. The Bible was written for all to read; but some portions are meant for the believer alone. Just as we should not read another person's mail, so we should seek to discover which Biblical mail is addressed to us. This passage is for believers only. In Scripture there is not even one promise for the unbeliever — there is only God's offer of salvation and His warning against eternal punishment.

What do we mean by confession? It does not mean to mumble a list of sins according to a prescribed form. Neither does it mean to recite one's past in public. I believe it is antibiblical for revival meetings to feature marathon confessions of private sin. There is no warrant in the Bible for public confession of private sin. Sometimes in a revival meeting even evangelicals fall under the sway of mass psychology and begin to dredge up the past, spouting forth lurid details with masterful pride. The greater the sin, the greater their apparent spirituality. After the meeting they return to their daily tasks and begin to sin again. Why? In an oral exercise touched with emotion, they made a profession of confession; it was not borne out by their lives. True confession affects daily conduct. When once we behold God's holiness and recognize our sinfulness, with Isaiah we shall cry, "I am a man of unclean lips, and I dwell in the midst of a people of unclean lips!" (Isa. 6:5).

True confession not only acknowledges past sins but it requires a new attitude toward sin: the believer must take sides with God against himself. True confession alters conduct for the better. To use a military figure, it demands unconditional surrender. We must come to God on His terms, determine to live for Him and decide to hate sin. These are the elements of true confession.

What is the purpose of confession as taught in the Word? It is the means which God has ordained to maintain fellowship with Himself. "God is light, and in him is no darkness at all" (1 John 1:5). When we commit sin, we break fellowship with God. By means of confession we keep short accounts with God. When we do wrong, we are to confess it immediately to the Father.

At the close of a telephone conversation a Christian woman put her hands to her face and said, "O Lord, my old nature broke out again! I have been gossiping!" Her maid overheard and said, "Whatcha doin', Missy?" The woman replied, "O Julie, I sinned, and I'm confessing it to the Lord!" Said the maid, "Is that what you does? Ah saves ma sins till night, and bunches 'em!" Whoever "saves 'em up till night" loses his day.

We are not to allow our sins to pile up. We are to keep the books balanced by coming instantly to God. This is the only way to peace, the only means to fellowship. This is the condition for blessing.

In the days when Israel turned away from the Lord, the prophet Hosea cried out, "Return, O Israel, to the Lord your God, for you have stumbled because of your iniquity. Take with you words and return to the Lord" (Hos. 14:1, 2). Likewise we must come with words to God. We must name the sin we have committed. We must admit that we willfully sinned against Him of our own accord. We must not try to blame someone else. Do not say, "There were two of us and we strayed into lust." Or, "There were three of us and we strayed into drunkenness." Or, "Our entire social set went into sin." Your part in any of these things was by your own choice. You took your eyes from the Lord; you stopped reading His Word which is a lamp for your feet and a light for your path. You grieved the Holy Spirit until He became silent and His voice no longer rebuked and warned you.

And in naming the sin that you have committed, don't try to call it by some lesser name or to speak in fuzzy generalizations. No matter what the details were, mention those details to God. Do not be satisfied with a general confession; be specific. A general confession is good to say in unison in public meetings, but when you are alone with God it is not enough to say, "I have erred and strayed from Thy way like a lost sheep. . . . I have left undone those things which I ought to have done; and I have done those things which I ought not to have done, and there is no health in me."

That is good for a start, but you must come down to cases: "Lord,

I began by flirting and ended by committing adultery." Or, "Lord, I began by borrowing money from the cash drawer until payday, but I got in over my head and finally stole it. I am a thief!" Or, "I wanted to be prominent in the conversation so I told malicious lies about an innocent person. I am guilty of slander." Or, "I hadn't studied for the examination so I cheated by looking over my neighbor's shoulder and copying from his paper." Or, "I wanted to put on a good front before my social set, so I went into debt for a mink coat and a high-priced car."

When you do this, God will bless you and cleanse you from *all* unrighteousness. He does this for the sake of Christ and because He is faithful and just. Christ died for us; He rose again, and sits at the Father's right hand making intercession for us. The Father sees the pledge of the blood, He hears the pleading of His Son, and He cannot turn us away. He is "faithful and just to forgive us our sins, and to cleanse us from all unrighteousness."

Clear understanding of this doctrine brings great blessing. Sin may enter my life, but my eternal welfare will not be affected. However, I hasten to confess the sin so that I shall not lose the privileges of fellowship. For the believer who understands the doctrine of confession, there is also abiding joy and continual access to the Father through the Son. His intercession assures our salvation. Nothing can be laid to our charge; we "are free from the law of sin and death."

Suppose you have killed a child with your car. Someone says to you, "I am terribly sorry for you! You are going to get the electric chair!" You would reply, "But it was an accident! I shall be charged with manslaughter, not murder!"

Believers will not be deprived of salvation because they sin, since Christ died and rose again for our justification. They may lose fellowship and blessing; but if they confess — unconditionally surrender — to Him, He will forgive and cleanse. It is impossible for God to send to hell anyone who has truly trusted in Christ.

But, you may ask, "What is meant by 'confess[ing] your faults to one another'?" (James 5:16). This passage, we believe, refers to public sin. The main thrust of James 5:15 does not concern divine healing but teaches the method of church discipline. In context, a man has fallen ill because he has committed a sin which is a public detriment to the church. He may confess his sin before the church and ask for prayer. This passage does not teach that God promises to heal every believer who becomes ill. Many faithful people in the Bible suffered maladies of which they were not healed, notably the Apostle Paul. He had a severe affliction but the Lord refused to heal him (2 Cor. 12:8,9). Yet few men in Scripture were more wonderfully used. We firmly believe that God brings a different type of illness upon those who flagrantly disregard His will. When they repent and confess, He forgives and heals.

Another question that arises is, "What about the 'sin unto death' mentioned in 1 John 5:16, 17?" John is warning believers of severe chastisement if they dare presume on God's grace in order to indulge in sin. God may chastise them with physical death, as if He were saying, "Since you persist in disobeying Me, I am removing you from service and am taking you out of life." But this penalty is only physical death, not the second death. Public confession of such sin wards off the judgment of premature death.

In order to maintain unbroken fellowship with God through our Lord Jesus Christ, we must confess sins as they occur. Let us keep short accounts with God, day by day conforming our conduct to His will so that we may be well pleasing to Him. If you are conscious that you have strayed from the paths of righteousness in which He desires to lead you, if you wish to renew fellowship with your heavenly Father, be assured that He misses your fellowship and longs to have you close to Himself once more. Get alone with Him and confess in detail all you have done; do not spare yourself. You will then know the joy of His forgiveness, His peace will fill your heart, and He will lead you in the paths of righteousness for His name's sake. These are the results of true confession.

Chapter Eighteen

MARKS OF TRUE DEVOTION

Standing by the mother of Jesus when our Lord was dying on the cross was Mary, the wife of Cleopas, whom tradition believes to have been the sister of Mary (John 19:25). Probably Cleopas, too, was in the group that watched the Savior die. To this pair, the aunt and uncle of the Lord Jesus — if we may accept the traditional story — was accorded a great honor.

On the morning of the resurrection Cleopas and Mary left Jerusalem for the strangest journey of their lives. It was a journey that needs to be traveled by every Christian. It started out in disbelief and sadness. It was a family sadness — their beloved sister had "lost" that strange Son of hers.

When they awakened that morning they heard astonishing news. Certain women reported that the tomb in which Jesus' body had been buried was empty and that angels had said that He was alive. Some of the men ran to the tomb and brought back a confirming report — the tomb was indeed empty. Nevertheless, Cleopas and Mary started for their home in Emmaus (Luke 24). They did not believe in Christ's resurrection; they were miserable. As they walked along the road discussing events of the preceding days, suddenly the Lord

Jesus Himself drew near to them. They did not recognize Him; they had last seen Him scarred and broken. His face was more marred than any man and His body more than any of the sons of men (Isa. 52:14).

He asked what they were talking about. "Cleopas answered him, Are you the only visitor to Jerusalem who does not know the things that have happened there in these days?" (Luke 24:18).

The Lord drew them out with the question, "What things?" for He was about to teach one of His greatest lessons. They told Him the story. How simple were the words on their lips! How full of misunderstanding! They answered the Lord that "Jesus of Nazareth, who was a prophet mighty in deed and word before God and all the people," had been delivered by the rulers to be condemned to death and had been crucified. And then came the artless confession that shows all that was in their minds, that reveals the cause of their blindness and of the blindness of all in their generation who did not accept Jesus as the Messiah. "We trusted that it had been he which should have redeemed Israel!" How ignorant they were of the plan of God, the ways of God and the Word of God! They were looking for triumph without sacrifice, for the feast of the Trumpets and the feast of the Tabernacles without the feast of the Passover. They thought that a Joshua could lead the people into the promised land before a Moses had led them out of Egypt.

And what had He done by dying and rising again? He had redeemed Israel and the whole world. But redeemed them from what? From sin and death. Oh, that! Poor Cleopas and his wife were looking for redemption from Rome. They would have been satisfied with a Messiah who brought down angels to chase all the Roman soldiers out of Palestine. Is it any wonder that Jesus said, "O foolish men, and slow of heart to believe all that the prophets have spoken!" (Luke 24:25). The unbelief of Israel was their failure to apply all prophecies of the Old Testament to the Messiah.

To this couple in these circumstances Jesus preached the first sermon of the Christian era. The date was the day of His resurrection. The place was a country road outside Jerusalem. The audience was composed of one Jewish peasant couple. The theme was, "Jesus Christ in the Old Testament." The searching question was asked,

"Was it not necessary that the Christ should suffer these things and enter into his glory?" (Luke 24:26). Clearly He was saying, "The Old Testament had to be fulfilled. You have it in your hands. All I have accomplished has been according to those Scriptures."

Christ died for our sins according to the Scriptures; He rose again the third day according to the Scriptures. He died as a Lamb, to cleanse us by pouring out His life in shedding His blood. Thus Leviticus 17:11 is the John 3:16 of the Old Testament: "For the life of the flesh is in the blood; and I have given it for you upon the altar to make atonement for your souls; for it is the blood that makes atonement, by reason of the life."

Christ began with the writings of Moses, and I have often wondered which of the passages He used. His audience was so spellbound that later they said, "Did not our hearts burn within us while he talked to us on the road, while he opened to us the scriptures?" (Luke 24:32). If you want the experience of the burning heart, look for the Lord Jesus in the Old Testament.

The trio reached the home of Cleopas, and the Lord took one step away as though He would go on. God is love, and He will not violate your heart. He wants you to love Him freely. Thus they stood; thus you may stand today. He will not move farther away unless you take a step away from Him. If you move toward Him, even slightly, if you breathe one sigh of hope or expectation, if your heart surges with desire for Him, He will come with you. "Draw near to God and he will draw near to you" (James 4:8). They constrained Him, saying, "Stay with us, for it is toward evening and the day is now far spent" (Luke 24:29).

Christ is so easily constrained!

Let that sentence stand by itself: Christ is so easily constrained!

Cleopas and his wife knew that here was no ordinary person. His vast knowledge of the Scriptures indicated that he was at least a famous Rabbi. Yet they did not hesitate to invite Him to share their food and spend the night in their home. Cleopas probably had to build a fire. Mary had to begin her work in a kitchen cold for many days. But finally everything was ready and they sat down to the table for what they thought was the beginning of a meal, but which turned out to be something so tremendous that I doubt whether they ate

much. There are times, as the Lord taught His disciples, that we have
meat to eat that others know not of (John 4:32).

As the three sat at the table, the Lord Jesus took bread and blessed
it and broke it and gave it to them. "And their eyes were opened and
they recognized him; and he vanished out of their sight" (Luke 24:
31). But not out of their hearts. He was there forevermore.

There was no consternation in the little house, but there was immediate decision. "They rose that same hour and returned to Jerusalem" (Luke 24:33). Recognition of the risen Lord Jesus Christ
always leads to decisive action. Cleopas and his wife immediately
desired to tell others about the risen Lord. How can we leave loved
ones in ignorance when we know the power and the presence of the
risen Lord? And if they already know about Him and we know about
Him, we must desire to communicate with each other. One of the
surest marks of the new birth is that we love the brethren. John
says, "We know that we have passed from death unto life, because
we love the brethren" (1 John 3:14).

It was already near evening when the trio had arrived at Emmaus.
There was certainly time consumed in preparing the meal. The mani-
festation and disappearance of Jesus must have occurred at the very
end of the day; perhaps darkness had already set in. The decision
to return to Jerusalem demanded courage as well as resolution, but
man and wife set out on the road. How different the return journey! They had left Jerusalem in despair; they had been joined by
Him who turned travel into wonder; and they were now returning full
of light, although they were walking in darkness. Every step must
have been filled with memory. Remember this rock? He stood with
His hand just there, as He told us that Jesus Himself was the Seed
of the woman. And here is the place where we stopped while He
told of Jesus as the Root, the Branch, the Lamb and the Lion.

And so it went. Hearts throbbing, hearts soaring, and then the
lights of Jerusalem. The narrow streets. Knocking at the door.
Cautious opening, and then joyful exclamations. It seems that those
of Jerusalem got their word in first. "The Lord has risen indeed,
and has appeared to Simon!" (Luke 24:34). Probably the Lord allowed this little phrase to be spoken first to give them the assurance
and courage to tell their lengthy story: "Then they told what had hap-

pened on the road, and how he was known to them in the breaking
of the bread" (Luke 24:35). While they were describing how
they recognized Him in the breaking of the bread, Christ Himself
stood in the room where the disciples were gathered.

There is no record of when Cleopas and Mary returned to Emmaus. The same night? The next day? Some time later? It makes
no difference. The home of Emmaus was never the same again. When
a married couple have seen the risen Lord Jesus Christ together, life
and home can never be the same again. This is the quintessence
of Christian marriage. In fact, any marriage that does not have this
factor in it falls short of being what God wants marriage to be. Christian marriage is the husband, the wife, and the Lord Jesus Christ.
Some time ago a young starry-eyed bride came to my wife and said,
"You know, the most wonderful thing about marriage is family worship. Isn't it wonderful!" And indeed it is. The more closely we
know the Lord, the more intimate we shall be with Him. The
time will come when we shall know Him in the breaking of the
bread at our table. We shall see Him in the closest intimacies of
life. Love will flow and overflow. It is only when we thus know Him
that we shall understand that "God is love, and he who abides in love
abides in God, and God abides in him" (1 John 4:16).

If you do not know the power of the resurrection, bid Him come
in to abide with you. He will; and you will experience the three
"openings" of Luke 24: First, "He opened the scriptures" (v. 32).
Next, when they saw Him take bread and bless it, "their eyes were
opened and they recognized him" (v. 31). When they rejoined the
other disciples and Jesus stood among them, He said, "These are my
words which I spoke to you, while I was still with you, that everything written about me in the law of Moses and the prophets and the
psalms must be fulfilled. Then he opened their minds to understand
the scriptures" (vv. 44, 45).

If you want the experience of the burning heart, look for the Lord
Jesus in the Old Testament. I do not know of a more wonderful
study. In Genesis 3, we see Him as the Seed of the woman who would
bruise the serpent's head, while His heel would be bruised. At Calvary, Christ did bruise Satan's head when He accomplished our redemption. In Genesis, too, He is the Seed of Abraham in whom all

the families of earth are blessed. The life of Joseph perfectly typi-
fied the Lord Jesus; the beloved' of his father, rejected by his brethren,
and exalted to be the savior of his people. In Exodus, Christ is pre-
figured by the passover lamb whose blood redeemed the first-born
and by the manna which fed the people day by day. And all the
furnishings of the Tabernacle spoke of Him. In Numbers He is the
Rock from which the water came forth. In Deuteronomy He is the
one whose everlasting arms support His people. Joshua met Him as
the captain of the Lord's host, while in the Book of Judges He appears
to the parents of Samson as the One whose name is Wonderful. The
Psalms tell of His suffering and eventual triumph. In Proverbs He
is the wisdom of God. Isaiah saw Him as the man of sorrows,
acquainted with grief, led as a lamb to the slaughter, pouring out His
soul unto death for the sins of His people. Daniel beheld Him as
the Ancient of days and as the great Stone which will crush the
nations. In Hosea He is the Son whom God called out of Egypt,
while Zechariah beholds Him riding into Jerusalem on a donkey, presenting Himself as the King of Israel. Zechariah also sees Him sold
for thirty pieces of silver. Lastly, Malachi sees Him as the Lord who
suddenly comes to His temple and as the Sun of Righteousness who
rises with healing in His wings. These are but a few of the many,
many Old Testament pictures and prophecies of the Lord Jesus
Christ.

When you open the Bible under the guidance of the Holy Spirit
and see your glorious Savior on every page, you will never be the
same again. Your heart will burn with true devotion to Him as you
read of His great love in coming to earth to be crucified and buried
for your sins. And your eyes will be opened when you see the risen
Lord who was raised again for your justification.